CONFRONTATION IN THE EAST

Confrontation in the East

A BACKGROUND BOOK

Douglas Hyde

DUFOUR EDITIONS

CHESTER SPRINGS, PENNSYLVANIA

CONTENTS

I

This is Confrontation

INDONESIAN troops and volunteers cross an invisible border which runs through some of the wildest country on earth and seek to establish guerrilla bases in the deep jungle on the other side. Malaysian and British troops hack their way through that same fiercely unyielding jungle in an attempt to get at them. To the Indonesians this is 'konfrontasi'. To the Malays it is 'konfrantasi'. To the British, and to most of the world, it is known as 'confrontation'.

A young Malaysian Chinese girl, loaded down with a Sten gun, ammunition and rations, a dagger at her belt, jumps terrified from an Indonesian troop-carrier, parachutes down into the area in which she has grown up, charged with the task of trying to form the nucleus of a guerrilla army which will convert her homeland into a battlefield. This, too, is confrontation.

A Malay nationalist, member of an extremist group, with little knowledge of politics and even less, it seems, of explosives, travels in a small sampan, hiding himself under a cargo of rubber, across the narrow straits which separate Indonesian islands from Singapore. Under cover of darkness he drags a sack of TNT up a jetty, then sets off in search of a railway bridge, a power station or a water pipeline which he can destroy. This also is confrontation.

* * *

South-East Asia is one of the world's more colourful areas. It is what Western tourists like to call 'exotic'. To the people who live there, of course, it is just 'home'. But we must not be surprised if political policies here are sometimes expressed in colourful terms and put into operation by colourful-sounding people. President Sukarno of Indonesia, for example, can talk of chewing up Malaysia and spitting out the bits. Some of the people involved in the practical application of his confrontation concept sound colourful too. There are, to name a few, Omar the crocodile hunter, Nordin bin Lemon the Malay prizefighter turned terrorist, Bambang Partono the diplomat who bought recruits for his cause and the anonymous 'mad bomber of Singapore'.

This is not a day-by-day record or history of Indonesia's confrontation of Malaysia. It is too early for such a book to be written. It is an attempt to provide some of the background, discover some of the roots of confrontation, and take a look at some of the people and some of the conditions that have made it possible. In particular it is concerned with those aspects of this dispute between two Asian countries which may have a relevance elsewhere.

For the fact is that this sort of confrontation could happen in any one of the developing continents. It would not be difficult to find the opposite number of either Indonesia or Malaysia in Africa, or, for that matter, in Latin America. Omar the crocodile hunter would be quite at home and almost equally happy stirring up trouble among the national minority from across the border in many an African country. Nordin bin Lemon has his opposites in plenty in the slums of other Asian cities. The 'mad bomber of Singapore' would have an already long tradition behind him were he a Latin American. And as for Bambang Partono—such people have been at work already in newly independent African countries, according to reports from the most authoritative sources.

It would be tragic, however, if a confrontation of this sort were to occur elsewhere. For it concerns new countries with neither human nor material resources to waste, where people desire only to be allowed to live in peace so that they may progress as quickly as possible, and where, one might hope, governments conscious that they represent the 'newly emergent forces' of today would work for a future more sane, more humane, than has been the past of the 'old-established forces' from whose rule they have at last been freed.

*   *   *

Weapons, ammunition, a parachute and a steel helmet surrounded small, bespectacled, mild-looking Dato Dr Ismail bin Abdul Rahman, Malaysian Minister of Home Affairs and Justice, as he addressed the United Nations Security Council in New York on September 9, 1964. In the name of his government he called on the Council to condemn Indonesia for 'international brigandage' and aggression and to enjoin her to 'desist from such activity'.

In the chair was Mr Platon D. Morozov, of the USSR. Around the table sat the representatives of China, France, the UK, USA, Brazil, Morocco, Norway, Bolivia, Czechoslovakia and the Ivory Coast. The story Dr Ismail had to tell them was one of bitter disillusionment. He reminded them of the close ties which his country had maintained with Indonesia going back to the days before World War II when both were colonial countries.

When the Indonesian people had fought for their independence from Dutch rule, Malaya, Singapore, Sabah and Sarawak (the states which now compose Malaysia) gave them material and moral support. Hundreds of their citizens went over to Indonesia to 'join our brethren and fight side by side with them'. Some laid down their lives for Indonesia. 'In those days and after,' said Dr Ismail sadly, 'Indonesian leadership was a source of inspiration and guidance to us.'

A special relationship had existed between the two countries. Indeed, a treaty of friendship concluded in 1959 remained the only one of its kind ever entered into by independent Malaya or the new Malaysia. But something had gone wrong. Despite the fact that the United Nations Secretary-General, U Thant, had ascertained that the Borneo states and Singapore wished to join Malaya in the broadened Federation of Malaysia, Indonesia had refused to accept this.

She had announced a military and economic 'confrontation' policy against Malaysia.

Indonesian Army infiltrators, both regulars and irregulars, had 'flooded into the Borneo states from across the 1,000 miles of jungle-infested border'. They had carried on a continuous series of hit-and-run raids 'from the safe sanctuary of their own part of Borneo'. But Indonesia had sought something more dramatic and damaging 'to sustain its revolutionary image in the eyes of its own people'. In a reckless gamble which at once enlarged the area of conflict and intensified the methods used, Indonesia, Dr Ismail said, had now moved forward to 'blatant aggression' by dropping three platoons of heavily armed paratroopers in a remote area of southern Malaysia.

This, he insisted, was an incident without parallel in peacetime relations and without precedent in history between two neighbouring sovereign states not at war, however ill-disposed towards each other they might be. He supported his allegations with a vast mass of documentary evidence to which he referred from time to time. Available for those who wanted to know more were exact details of every raid into Malaysian territory and of broadcasts from radio stations on islands of the Indonesian archipelago aimed at stirring up racial hatred between the different communities who make up Malaysia's multi-racial population. Briefly, on the table before him appeared the weapons, ammunition, parachute and steel helmet. These, on the stern insistence of the presiding Soviet delegate, were hurriedly and a little nervously removed by UN officials.

Those who had worked with Dr Ismail in the preparation of his country's case to the Security Council no doubt expected Indonesia's representative to try in some way either to deny everything or, possibly, to explain it away. What no one expected was the line that Indonesia actually took.

In reply to Dr Ismail's charge of 'blatant and inexcusable aggression', Dr Sudjarwo Tjondronegoro, Indonesia's

Deputy Foreign Minister, said it was up to Malaysia to decide whether she wanted peace or war with Indonesia. He did not deny that 'Indonesian volunteers' had entered Malaysian territory in Sarawak and Sabah. He made no bones about it. 'They have been fighting there for some time,' he said. This was no secret. And, in the absence of a peaceful solution to the conflict between Malaysia and Indonesia, 'the fighting activities on both sides could only become aggravated or even escalate'.

'And now,' he went on, 'this fighting has spread to other areas in Malaysia, such as Malaya. Why is Malaysia so greatly concerned now that it requests a meeting of the Security Council? Why was it not equally concerned much earlier when the fighting broke out in Sarawak and Sabah, which is also a part of Malaysia?'

As if to make it abundantly plain to all present that Indonesia not only did not deny, but also actually prided itself on having done all that Dr Ismail had claimed, he flatly asserted that 'as a matter of fact, the fighting now in Malaya is on a very small scale compared to the magnitude of the fighting in Sarawak and Sabah'.

Hostilities between Indonesia and Malaya, involving incursions into each other's territory, he said, had been going on for some time. In fact, Indonesia suffered incursions and subversions from the territories which now form the present Malaysia, back in the days when they were British colonies.

Dr Sudjarwo threw down the gauntlet before those whom he described as representatives of the 'old-established forces'. 'Mr President,' he cried, 'what do we mean by "aggression"? Even the United Nations has not been successful in finding an agreed definition for it. Indonesia's acts, pursued by volunteers for the cause of freedom against neo-colonialism, can certainly not be termed "aggression".'

Like Dr Ismail, he recalled the treaty of friendship which the two countries had concluded only a few years ago. 'But, alas, soon it also appeared that the chain of British colonialism in Malaya, supported by the presence of Britain's powerful military bases in Singapore and elsewhere, had not been weakened much, let alone broken.'

Tunku Abdul Rahman, the Malaysian Prime Minister, he continued, seemed to forget that the confrontation policy and the guerrilla activities 'are only the consequence, not the cause, of the Malaysian conflict. Its cause is the existing political dispute.'

He filled in the background to Indonesia's own attitude and actions. Indonesia, he said, had suffered much since she achieved her independence from colonialism and imperialism. 'It was colonialism and imperialism which separated our peoples, artificially divided our great family into differing units.' South-East Asia had been the playground of colonialism and imperialism in the past. Then, using the terms which express the concept which is at the very heart of Indonesia's revolution, her foreign policy and her approach to the mid-twentieth century, Dr Sudjarwo said: 'The new emerging revolutionary forces meet strong opposition from the old-established forces of the world which want to maintain their old domination, politically, economically, and militarily or strategically, for as long as possible.'

In the past Indonesia had had to face opposition primarily from Netherlands colonialism. 'In the process, we learned something dear—that to attain genuine independence, genuine freedom, one has to struggle and suffer, to fight, even to die if necessary.' Today, years after gaining her independence, Indonesia still felt herself to be confronted by imperialism although from a different direction. The new Malaysia, with its British bases, had permitted itself to become the tool of the old forces. Hence this new confrontation.

When it came to the vote, nine of the eleven members of the Security Council voted in favour of a Norwegian resolution which deplored the landings of Indonesian paratroopers in Malaysia. The two who voted against were from Communist Czechoslovakia and the Soviet Union. Predictably, the resolution was vetoed by Russia. The Indonesians went home satisfied. They had stood up to the imperialists in their own stronghold and had demonstrated that they had a strong, sympathetic ally in the Soviet Union. The Malaysians for their part could return claiming a moral victory.

*　　*　　*

In Bangkok a few days after this debate I talked with an information officer of the Indonesian embassy in Thailand. He asked me whether I understood his country's case as put to the Security Council. As I understood it, I replied, Indonesia was not denying anything, or apologizing for anything. The Republic of Indonesia's representative had in effect said: 'We fought against colonialism in the past and we are fighting it in its new form in Malaysia today. That is the situation whether you like it or not and you must not expect us to go around apologizing for what we are doing.' The information officer agreed with that summary.

Indonesia, I went on, had good reason to know that she could expect no love, no sympathy, from the Western Powers for what she was doing. She had therefore decided that the best thing in the circumstances was to disregard Western feelings and talk to the people of Asia, Africa and Latin America, where the memory of colonialism dies hard and fear of neo-colonialism is very real. Since Indonesia's belief was that ultimately the new emerging forces must prevail, Dr Sudjarwo had understandably addressed his message to them and not to 'the old-established forces of this world'.

The information officer, a man of few words, smiled his appreciation and agreement.

2

The Confronters

'PLEASE tell us what to do. The Dutch taught us nothing.' This is what the visitor to Indonesia heard over and over again during the first ten years that followed the achievement of independence. By 1960 one heard it occasionally, but less often. By 1961 Indonesia was becoming sufficiently sure of herself for the public expression of such sentiments to be regarded as humiliating. People might be queueing for rice and cloth in Djakarta, the basic necessities of life might be in short supply, but the visitor was likely to be made as much aware of national pride as of poverty.

Indonesia today can only be understood if you approach her past with sympathy and understanding. Like the majority of other Asian lands, Indonesia has a colonial past, and, to a far greater extent than is the case elsewhere, that colonial past is still with her. Her history as a colony goes back to the days when a small handful of nations of the West believed, almost incredibly, that they had a right—perhaps even a God-given one—to divide the world between them and to rule it for evermore.

For three and a half centuries this large group of islands with its huge population and its immense natural wealth was ruled from thousands of miles away by the tiny Netherlands. From 1619 right down to the end of World War II there was practically non-stop opposition to colonial rule. There was, for example, full-scale war in Java from 1825 to 1830. In Sumatra a war which began in 1873 lasted for thirty-five years, till the last of the guerrillas surrendered in 1908. By the time the Dutch occupied the island of Bali in 1906 the first nationalist movements were already in existence. For 350 years they had tried to 'pacify' Indonesia yet by the time the job was completed, in so far as it ever was completed, Indonesian nationalism of the modern variety was already on the move.

Unlike some other colonial Powers, the Dutch did not just send in enough of their own nationals to rule the country; they settled there in large numbers. There were a quarter of a million Dutch and Dutch-Eurasians in Indonesia before World War II, forming something which came close to being a self-contained community. On the eve of World War II, the central government employed 73,354 persons; of these 79·1 per cent were Indonesians, but of that group all but 9 per cent were in the lowest possible positions. Of the administrative personnel 92·2 per cent were Dutch.

Modern Indonesian nationalism at first took the form of a social and cultural movement. Some of the earliest nationalist organizations were Islamic; some of the nationalist leaders in the days before World War I were self-proclaimed, though not always orthodox, Marxists. To this day the nationalist movement retains its Islamic and Marxist wings and President Sukarno's revolutionary thought draws both on religion and on Marxism.

The Japanese occupation of Indonesia during World War II gave the nationalists their chance. The mass of the people rejoiced to see the Western colonialists so quickly and so humiliatingly defeated. But, like the people in other parts of Asia, they were soon appalled by the methods used by the Japanese. This did not stop them from using the situation for nationalistic ends. The Japanese were willing to exploit expressions of anti-Western sentiment for their own purposes and the nationalists were happy to use any opportunities for organization which the Japanese provided.

During the occupation, Sukarno and Hatta, the best known of the nationalist leaders, collaborated with the Japanese, but not because they had any love for Japanese imperialism. At the same time, other nationalists operated clandestinely, trying to make an end of Japanese rule even as they worked also to ensure that there should be no return to the hated Western colonial rule. There is no reason to doubt that both groups, for their own equally good nationalist reasons, took the line they did.

When the war ended, the Dutch assumed that they could return to pre-war conditions. They met with bitter opposition. There was intermittent armed conflict from 1945 to 1949. The Republic came into existence against a background of 'police actions', revolts, guerrilla war and scorched earth. It was from such a background, too, that Sukarno gradually emerged as the father-figure of the revolution.

It was the misfortune of many of the new Asian and African countries that after years of struggle against colonial rule they at last gained their independence in a period when the world was divided into two camps, and in which independence had at best to be qualified. Even as the old flags came down and the new flags went up, the new governments were approached by great Powers of both camps and immediately asked to commit themselves to one or the other. Having freed themselves from years of unwilling attachment to one Power they were now expected willingly to identify themselves with a group of Powers instead. This was more than many of them could tolerate.

Understandably, Indonesia, very conscious of her own colonial past, opted from the start for non-alignment. The attempt to avoid being tied to the West has decisively influenced Indonesian foreign policy and the thinking of the Indonesian leaders ever since.

*   *   *

Four names dominate the Indonesian political scene today. President Sukarno, whose position is unique; Foreign Minister Subandrio, and General Nasution, Chief of Staff, who together put Sukarno's policies into action in the political and military fields; and D. N. Aidit, leader of the Communist Party (PKI) who, with nearly three million members behind him, has the largest organized following apart from Sukarno himself.

Sukarno—or 'Bung' (Brother) Karno, as he now likes to be called—has always seen himself as a man of the people, a champion of the underprivileged. He has called himself the champion of the proletariat, but his social origin is bourgeois by Asian standards.

The future president was born in East Java in 1901. His father was a Moslem Javanese schoolteacher who became a member of the Theosophical Society. His mother was a Hindu Balinese. This mixed religious background has undoubtedly contributed to his tolerant approach to people of all religions and none. Sukarno rarely makes a speech without some reference to God and he is just as likely to make an important political statement at a Catholic gathering as at a Moslem one or, for that matter, at a national congress of the PKI.

He became known as a fiery orator while he was still a student, and within a couple of years of graduating he was chairman of the Bandung Study Club, from which the Indonesian Nationalist Organization was formed in 1927. The following year this became the Partai National Indonesia (Indonesian Nationalist Party) whose aim was complete independence. In 1929 he was charged along with others with planning a rebellion and given a four-year sentence which was later reduced to two. Like many another future president of recent times, he was made a 'prison graduate', a martyr for the cause of nationalism and anti-colonialism.

He was arrested again in 1933, along with his fellow nationalist leaders Hatta and Sjahrir, and was not released until the Japanese arrived in 1942. Sukarno had by now had plenty of time to think about political theories and policies but very little opportunity to put them into practice. To this day he gives the impression that he is more interested in ideas than in their actual implementation, which, in effect, he leaves to others.

During World War II, because he collaborated with the Japanese, Moscow Radio called him a quisling, but within months of the ending of the war even communists in far-away Britain, as I well recall, were being told, 'Sukarno is all right'. This was based in part upon his willingness to describe himself as a Marxist, and partly upon the somewhat arrogant belief that because of his tolerant approach communists should not find it difficult to manipulate him.

In 1945, when the Japanese occupation was clearly about to end, Sukarno made a speech announcing the *Pantja Sila*, the Five Principles. These principles (faith in one God, humanity, nationalism, representative government and social justice) are still the declared basis of the ideology of the Indonesian revolution. That revolution, Sukarno believes, is a continuing one. It did not end with the ending of Dutch rule. In theory it must continue until the Five Principles have become realities. Certainly Sukarno and his spokesmen argue today that it must continue until colonialism and neo-colonialism are ended and until Asians are free to provide Asian solutions to Asian problems.

Indonesia's search for a suitable form of representative government and for social justice was first expressed in a not very successful attempt at Western-style democracy. This was brought to an end in 1957 when President Sukarno proclaimed his own 'guided democracy'. In March 1960 the elected Parliament was dissolved by presidential decree and was replaced by one composed of members appointed by the President himself.

A political manifesto, for which Sukarno claimed credit, was to provide the political basis for the new guided democracy. Its wording was such that nationalists, religious believers and communists alike could all feel that it was intended for them. But it seemed obvious to anyone who knew the way the communists work that they would put their own Marxist-Leninist interpretation on it and would condemn as traitors to the principles of guided democracy all those who did not interpret it their way. This is what they did and to this day are still doing.

This ability to talk in terms acceptable to all the main groups upon whom he depends has so far been President Sukarno's strength. It could in certain circumstances prove to be his downfall. For steadily over the years the communists seek to commit him more and more deeply to the Marxist side of his utterances and to isolate those who take up an anti-Marxist position by branding them, not as anti-Marxist but as anti-Sukarno.

Sukarno has nevertheless shown extraordinary skill in balancing one political vested interest against another. In this he has shown himself to be an unusually adroit politician, judged by any standards. It is probably fair to say that the President aims to be recognized as something more than an adroit politician. He wants to be acknowledged as a world statesman. As the years pass, and he becomes increasingly concerned with his health and advancing age, this becomes an ever-increasing preoccupation.

His one hope of achieving this ambition rests on whether he can have himself accepted as leader of and spokesman for the non-aligned nations, the 'third world'. Since the death of Pandit Nehru the chair has been empty. It is Sukarno's misfortune that just as the 'two worlds' concept has become less meaningful since the death of John Foster Dulles so today the 'third world' concept is already beginning to lose its significance. The existence of a number of non-aligned nations does not in itself necessarily constitute a basis for a third bloc, least of all at a time when the 'East' and 'West' blocs no longer appear to be as monolithic as they once did. And there are, incidentally, other nationalist leaders, such as President Gamal Abdel Nasser of Egypt and President Kwame Nkrumah of Ghana, who probably feel that if there is to be a third bloc they have at least as much right as Sukarno to lead it.

*　　*　　*

21

Dr Subandrio, President Sukarno's Foreign Minister, is a younger man—he was born in 1914—who also since his student days has been a militant nationalist. When Sukarno was working overtly for nationalist aims during the Japanese occupation, Subandrio, a Javanese surgeon, was working with underground groups. He worked in the Ministry of Information in the first days of independence and is still intensely propaganda-minded. Having been the Republic's ambassador in Britain and in the Soviet Union, he can claim to have some knowledge of both 'West' and 'East'.

Whilst Dr Subandrio has from time to time shown himself willing to criticize President Sukarno in private, he has none the less remained very close to him and increasingly reflects his mind. Since he has no party behind him, Subandrio depends for his future political career almost entirely upon the President's goodwill.

To him, as to Sukarno himself, the revolution takes precedence over everything else. For this reason, and because he sees confrontation as the current expression of the revolution, he is prepared to urge that social progress and economic well-being must take second place to national glory.

* * *

In September 1964 Dr Subandrio bluntly declared that the nation was required to hold back the desire for a better economic life, in the interests of the Indonesian revolution. 'We are indeed striving for the improvement of the standard of living of the people', he said, 'but this is not the immediate goal' which is 'to heighten the endurance of the revolution in the military, political and social fields.' President Sukarno took the same line at the Second Conference of Non-aligned Nations in Cairo the following month. That the people of this poverty-stricken yet potentially wealthy new country should for one moment accept such a policy is a tribute to the hold which President Sukarno has on the public imagination and also to Dr Subandrio's skill as a propagandist.

On September 15, 1964, I talked to a sergeant of the Indonesian army who a few days earlier had been parachuted into Johore State charged with the task of trying to establish a guerrilla base in the Malayan jungle. Now he was a prisoner.

He told me that the first time he ever went into action was against the communists during their rising at Madiun in 1948. 'They killed almost everyone in our camp, which meant nearly all my friends,' he added. I asked him if he had any feelings about having been sent into action in Malaysia by a government which now had a communist in the Cabinet. He replied that he did not like it, then added, 'But I am a regular soldier and I am supposed to have no politics.'

General Abdul Haris Nasution, Minister of Defence and Commander of the Armed Forces, who, I suppose it may be said, was indirectly responsible for the sergeant's being there, is both a soldier and a politician. Unlike Dr Subandrio he has behind him a powerful, organized force, the Army, to support him in his position in the government.

Nasution, who is a Moslem, was born in 1918. He started his working life as a schoolteacher, but later attended the Royal Netherlands Military Academy in Bandung and was commissioned as a subaltern in the Royal Netherlands Indies army in 1941. He was captured by the Japanese the following year and later worked for them. In the early years after World War II he led commandos in the fight against the attempt to restore colonial rule to Indonesia. It was then that he learned guerrilla warfare, a subject on which he was later to establish himself as an authority.

The communists staged their revolt at Madiun, East Java, in September 1948, a time when Hatta, a moderate nationalist, was Prime Minister. The revolt weakened the infant Republic. It encouraged the Dutch to launch another 'police action', during which Sukarno and Hatta were exiled. Colonel Nasution, as he was at that time, was above all else a nationalist. He had no love for communists, who were prepared to endanger the country's independence in pursuit of their own aims. It is just possible that, like the captured sergeant in Johore, he draws no inspiration from the thought that communists are now in the Government and in the Cabinet itself.

Despite his devotion to the revolution, Nasution was under a shadow at one time. In October 1952 he was suspended along with a number of his supporters after they had led demonstrations calling for the dissolution of Parliament. Some of the officers urged Sukarno to take dictatorial power; Nasution wanted a military junta. It took another army revolt, this time a more serious one which Nasution opposed, to bring him back into favour again. Between 1958 and 1961 a rebellion, which took the form of a number of regionalist revolts in Sumatra, occurred within the Army itself. Nasution and his senior officers were provided with the opportunity to demonstrate their loyalty to the Government and also their superiority over the rebels. In July 1959 Nasution was brought into the inner Cabinet as Minister for Defence and Security.

Partly because of the emergency conditions in which the Indonesian army has grown up, partly because its leaders still feel themselves to be nationalists and revolutionaries, Nasution's army has not confined itself to normal military activities. For years it consciously tried to move into those fields of activity which would otherwise be left wide open to the PKI, its rival within the National Front. The communists were organizing co-operatives; the Army quickly moved into the rural areas to organize co-operatives too. The Communist Party showed signs of preparing for an agitation on some social question. The Army would attempt to remove the cause of the agitation. Some of the best of the army officers saw themselves as being in direct personal competition, man for man, with the top communist leaders.

The revolt in Sumatra, which gave Nasution his chance to come back into favour, enabled the communists to rehabilitate themselves in the eyes of the public too. By strongly supporting the fight against the rebel officers they lived down the memory of Madiun, which since 1948 had hung like a mill-stone round their necks. In recent years they have succeeded in infiltrating the lower ranks of the Army itself and so represent a constant threat to the position of non-communist nationalists like General Nasution. The communists were once Nasution's enemies in the field; they are certainly his army's greatest rivals today.

*   *   *

Dipa Nasantara Aidit was born in 1922. This makes him one of the youngest communist leaders in the world—or at any rate of the larger communist parties.

Aidit moved up into leading positions in the PKI (Partai Kommunis Indonesia) in the years when the party was trying to recover from the consequences of Madiun. No one could have done more to assist it to live down the memory of that abortive revolt which led to its condemnation by the masses and was followed by years of political isolation. Aidit's promotion to the top position in January 1951 expressed a determination on the part of the party to reject the old, narrow sectarian approach to communism, and the desire that its appeal should be broadened by giving it a more genuinely Indonesian appearance. His analysis of the party's ills gave him the support of all those—and they were by now the majority—who recognized that the party must be brought out of its self-created ghetto or continue as a small, largely rejected minority.

In 1952 the party's membership was just under 8,000. By December 1963 Aidit could claim $2\frac{1}{2}$ million party members, with another $1\frac{1}{2}$ million members of the Pemuda Ra'ayat (Young Communist League), over 7 million members of communist-led peasant unions, and a total of 13 million members of 'mass' organizations—there are many million members of the powerful, communist-led trade unions which control nearly 75 per cent of the country's industrial labour force.

All this makes the PKI the biggest and most successful communist party of the non-communist world. It has gone further than any other in adapting itself to local conditions, traditions and culture. The Italians, with the second largest communist party, come second in adaptation, too. Both, interestingly enough, have had to adapt themselves to a largely religious culture.

The Indonesian's natural tendency towards toleration has doubtless helped this process. But the honours must go to Aidit, whose leadership of the party has been characterized by imagination and a lack of rigidity exceptional among communists. If President Sukarno has to walk the tightrope between the Army and the PKI, Aidit has to walk several tightropes. He must maintain a balance between dialectical materialism and Islam, between communist internationalism and Indonesian nationalism, and between Sukarno's guided democracy and communism.

Aidit is intelligent, sensitive, likeable and approachable. His private life is austere, but he mixes easily. He is flexible, yet never loses sight of the communist goal. For example, at the height of the campaign for the invasion of West Irian into which the PKI had thrown everything it had, he reminded his followers that it was American imperialism which was and must remain 'enemy number one'. And again repeatedly during the campaign to 'crush Malaysia' he has told his followers that though Malaysian neo-colonialism may be their immediate target it is American penetration of the Indonesian economy which is the bigger and continuing threat.

When Aidit supports Sukarno he does so because he believes that this serves the cause of communism best. When he identifies himself with the Indonesian revolution it is with an eye to the coming communist revolution. When he supports Sukarno's guided democracy—which its critics say is so authoritarian and paternalistic as to be a near-dictatorship—it is in the belief that it can be made to hasten the coming of a communist-controlled Indonesian People's Democracy. The discussion material issued under Aidit's leadership for the Sixth National Congress of the Communist Party of Indonesia in 1958 made this quite clear. 'Once the Indonesian revolution, which is national and democratic in character, has achieved complete victory,' it said, 'the duty of the PKI will then be to take the necessary steps to realize a system of socialism and a system of communism in Indonesia. . . .'

★　★　★

Indonesia is a country that is as long as the distance from London to the Caucasus and is composed of 10,000 islands, 5,000 of which are inhabited. Within that territory live 103 million people. Of these, 63 million are in Java, the island on which Djakarta, the capital, is situated; 16 million live in Sumatra, 4,200,000 in Kalimantan (Indonesian Borneo) and something less than 1 million, mainly Papuans, in West Irian (West New Guinea).

Jutting down from the Asian mainland and into the South China Sea, just across the narrow Straits of Malacca from Sumatra, is the Malay Peninsula, at the tip of which lies the small but important island of Singapore. The Straits between the two countries are so narrow that the lights of Singapore and Malaya may easily be seen at night from Indonesian soil. It is a mere half-hour's trip in a fast motor launch from Indonesia's Rhio Islands to the coast of Johore State in South Malaya. Looking out across the sea from a Singapore hill-top it is practically impossible to decide which are Malaysia's offshore islands and which Indonesia's.

Across the water, and about as far from Singapore as they are from Djakarta, are Sarawak and Sabah in northern Borneo or, as the Indonesians call it, North Kalimantan. These are the two former British territories which, along with Singapore, joined Malaya to form the new Malaysia in September 1963 simultaneously with achieving their independence.

Thus Indonesia runs scoop-shaped round Malaysia, 'confronting it' geographically on three sides. This is very relevant to Indonesia's political confrontation of Malaysia. Equally relevant is the fact that Malaysia has a population of 10 million—just under one-tenth of Indonesia's.

3

The Confronted

BECAUSE so many had talked of it for so long, it is difficult to trace who first suggested the formation of a Greater Malaysia. Malaya was already a federation of a number of different states and an enlargement of this grouping would clearly add to the chances of survival of four other small, neighbouring states which were due for independence— Singapore, Sarawak, North Borneo (known locally as Sabah) and Brunei. The idea is, in any case, too obvious and has too many roots in the past for any one individual to be able to claim credit for it. There is a close ethnic relationship between the indigenous people of the entire area—Malays, Ibans (Dyaks), Kayans, Kenyahs, Kadazans, Muruts and others.

The union of some of these territories was discussed at the turn of the century. But in those days communications were poor and the difficulties of administering areas divided from each other by sea were real. The coming of the air age opened up possibilities for federation which could not have existed in the past.

There were already close links between all the territories concerned. The need for a merger or some form of federation between Malaya and Singapore was obvious. The whole of the history of the two areas was inextricably bound up. And, more important for present and future needs, so too were their trade and their economic life. Malaya, Singapore, Sarawak, Sabah and Brunei were linked together in a single currency system administered by a Currency Board composed of representatives of all five territories. It was no surprise to any traveller in the area, therefore, to discover that even after Malayan independence in 1957 the common currency continued to be used. The 'Malayan dollar' was known for its soundness all over the world. 'Board of Commissioners of Currency, Malaya and British Borneo', said the inscription on notes and coins.

Because all the states concerned had been under British rule in one form or another they had a common tradition of law and justice, and a similar system of administration. In world organizations and international gatherings they were often represented by a single delegation drawn from them all. There was a constant exchange of ideas.

Within the Left-wing movement a special relationship had for years existed between socialist and trade union organizations in the various territories. There were close links between the early trade union movements of Malaya and of Singapore. Union organizers went from Singapore to Sarawak, North Borneo and Brunei to assist with the birth and growth of unions there. The socialists of the five territories maintained close contact with each other. A single communist party served both Malaya and Singapore. The founder of the underground communist organization of Sarawak received his inspiration from Singapore and was given his training there, and, earlier, the Communist Party of Malaya accepted responsibility for preparing the way for the communist movement in the North Borneo territories.

It was Tunku Abdul Rahman, the Malayan Prime Minister, who first made formal reference to Malaysia as a practical possibility. In a speech to pressmen in Singapore on May 27, 1961, he said: 'Malaya today as a nation realizes that she cannot stand alone. Sooner or later, Malaya must have an understanding with Britain and the peoples of the territories of Singapore, North Borneo, Brunei and Sarawak.' The speech received wide publicity, and action soon followed.

A Malaysia Solidarity Consultative Committee was established in August 1961 in order to examine what would be involved in the practical application of the Malaysian concept. This committee was composed of representatives of the peoples of the territories concerned. The Malayan government informed the Indonesian government of its intentions and was told that Indonesia had no objections.

In an address to the General Assembly of the United Nations on November 20, 1961, Dr Subandrio, Indonesia's Foreign Minister, said: 'We are not only disclaiming the territories outside the former Netherlands East Indies, though they are of the same island, but—more than that—when Malaya told us of its intention to merge with the three [sic] British Crown Colonies of Sarawak, Brunei and British North Borneo as one Federation, we told them that we had no objections and that we wished them success with this merger so that everyone might live in peace and freedom.

'For the sake of clarification, I may tell this Assembly that three-quarters of the island of Borneo is Indonesian territory, while the remainder constitutes the aforementioned three [sic] British Crown Colonies. Naturally, ethnologically and geographically speaking, this British part is closer to Indonesia than, let us say, to Malaya. But we still told Malaya that we had no objection to such a merger, based upon the will for freedom of the peoples concerned.'

A week earlier Dr Subandrio had expressed similar sentiments in a letter to the *New York Times* (November 13, 1961). He wrote:

'As an example of our honesty and lack of expansionist intent, one-fourth of our island of Kalimantan (Borneo) consisting of three Crown Colonies of Great Britain, is now becoming the target of the Malayan government for a merger. Of course, the people there are ethnologically and geographically very close to the others living in the Indonesian territory. Still, we do not show any objection towards this Malayan policy of merger. On the contrary, we wish the Malayan government well if it can succeed with this plan.'

There was nothing surprising at the time about the Indonesian government's attitude as outlined by Dr Subandrio in November 1961. It seemed fair, reasonable and obvious enough. Relations between Indonesia and Malaya had normally been good. Malay nationalists had drawn much of their inspiration from Indonesia. Malay intellectuals had gone to university there. The treaty of friendship concluded between the two countries in 1959 expressed this special relationship.

When Dr Subandrio, on behalf of his government, wished the project well, he knew that in Malaya and Singapore, with which the Borneo territories could unite, were established British military and naval bases and that by agreement those bases might remain there for many years. This was not raised as an objection by Indonesia's political leaders. In November 1961 relations between the Republic of Indonesia and the Chinese People's Republic were bad. Indonesia at that time was concerned for her own security. An Army spokesman in Djakarta told me at the time that the Army welcomed 'Greater Malaysia', as it was then called, because this would mean the continued presence of British bases which would help to ensure stability in the area.

Dr Subandrio's line was what might have been expected too because Indonesia was and is deeply committed to opposition to colonialism everywhere. Particularly since the Bandung Conference of 1955, she had enjoyed a reputation in the Afro-Asian countries for being the implacable enemy of imperialism, anxious to assist any country towards its independence. The formation of the new Malaysia promised to be a means by which four territories would quickly reach the end of colonial rule.

*   *   *

It became part of Indonesia's case against Malaysia that the Malayans never had to fight to get their freedom. Indonesians, who had to carry on a long, protracted struggle against the Dutch imperialists, are steeled-in-the-fire anti-colonialists; the Malayans, having achieved independence by peaceful means, are not.

There were purely local factors which inhibited the growth

of a nation-wide nationalist movement in Malaya. These included the almost equally balanced, multi-racial population, with the Chinese forming the majority in the cities and Malays in the rural areas; and the division of the country into states with different histories and different forms of government.

The Indonesian nationalists, led by Sukarno, had virtually no alternative but to fight to achieve national freedom by force of arms. It can be argued that the British created a somewhat similar situation in Kenya and Cyprus. In Malaya, however, they made it possible for the country to achieve independence and for Tunku Abdul Rahman to reach power by peaceful, democratic processes. To have taken the bloody road when a peaceful one was open to them would have been sheer lunacy on the part of the Malayan leaders. These are facts of history and they have a bearing on present events.

When the war in the Pacific ended, independence was in the air. The Western colonialists were discredited. In the disturbed conditions that existed in the first post-war years there were undoubtedly some Malays and many more Malayan Chinese who were ready to fight the British with guns if independence were too long delayed.

Some of the more militant Left Malay nationalists who might have been expected to take a leading part in such a struggle were drawn instead into the insurrection started by the communists in 1948. Consequently their struggle became merged with that of the communists. They came to be identified in both the public and the official mind with communism and the communist struggle for power. It was not only Indonesian nationalists who gave their lives for independence. There were Malayan nationalists who shed their blood in the same cause. But it is part of their tragedy that, deceived by the communists, they marched behind the wrong banner. And they fought and died unnecessarily. The coming of independence was postponed rather than hastened by their struggle.

When in the early days it was thought that the insurrection was genuinely being fought for national liberation, significant sections of the public either supported it or viewed it from a position of benevolent neutrality. But because they were short of arms and materials the communist leaders resorted increasingly to the use of terror. Public opinion turned against them and, inevitably, those associated with them were discredited, too. Both the colonial Power and the ordinary Malayan people came to have equally good though different reasons for wishing to see the insurrection defeated.

The ending of the revolt meant the opening of the way to independence. For it had undoubtedly postponed the end of colonial rule, just as it had also slowed down the country's development. Freedom came in the end not by the gun but by discussion and negotiation at the conference table.

Since *Merdeka* (freedom) the Malayan government's record in identifying itself with the oppressed and dissociating itself from the oppressors is as good as any. Malaya played a leading rôle in the anti-apartheid moves which led to South Africa's exit from the British Commonwealth. She has consistently raised her voice against racial discrimination everywhere. When Mr Winston Field's white-dominated government in Rhodesia threatened in 1964 to grab a form of independence which would prolong the white minority rule the Malaysian government was one of the first to come out against it.

The argument that the Tunku and his colleagues are stooges of the colonial Powers is weakened by the fact that, like Indonesia, Malaysia refused to join the South-East Asia Treaty Organization.

* * *

A majority of the population of the Malay Peninsula live within a few miles of the coast; a very large part of the rest of the country remains jungle-covered. Much of it is mountainous. Large areas are still unexplored. But in this small country a number of different races have settled over the years.

Indians came in the fifth century AD; Chinese traders began to arrive in the fourteenth and fifteenth centuries. In the sixteenth century came the Europeans. Malacca, on the coast, was captured by the Portuguese, but in the next century fell to the Dutch. The British established a foothold in Penang in the eighteenth century and in the other ten Malay states during the following century. In the nineteenth century, too, Chinese began to arrive in large numbers. By the early twentieth century, with the development of tin mining and the cultivation of rubber, they and the Indians were flooding in to work in the tin mines and on the rubber estates.

By 1961 the country's population was estimated at 7,232,000, made up of 3,260,000 indigenous people (Malayans, Indonesians of immigrant stock and a few primitive jungle-dwellers), 2,670,000 Chinese, 813,000 Indians and Pakistanis and 129,000 others. Here, then, was a modern, multi-racial community in which each has its own religion, language, culture and quite distinct traditions.

Multi-racial communities tend to be explosive in the modern world. British Guiana is an example of just how bitter racial conflict can become, particularly when the racial and party political patterns follow the same lines.

Malaya has for long been an encouraging example of the way in which very dissimilar peoples can live side by side in peace. The Malays and the Chinese—the two largest groups—could hardly be less alike, yet there were practically no racial incidents involving Malays and Chinese throughout the British period. Nor were there any until confrontation began. Indeed, the visitor to Malaya is invariably struck by the exceptionally friendly relationships which exist between the various sections of the community, and with the friendliness of the people generally.

Right up to the beginning of World War II no national political parties existed with the exception of the Malayan

Communist Party and it is doubtful whether this justified the description of 'national' since it was at that time exclusively Chinese and owed its main inspiration to China.

By the time political parties were beginning to come into existence, immediately after the end of the war, Britain was already ridding herself of her colonies and it was clearly only a matter of time before Malaya would be given its independence. The political organizations which emerged followed communal lines. The United Malay National Organization (UMNO), of which Tunku Abdul Rahman was to become leader, spoke for the majority of the Malay population; the Chinese had their Malay Chinese Association (MCA) and the Indians their Malay Indian Congress (MIC).

This form of political organization along communal lines might well have led to trouble had it not been that the leaders of the three groups got together to form a single alliance, which in due course was to form Malaya's first independent government. Outside the alliance were various socialist groups, the most significant of which were the Malayan Labour Party and Partai Ra'ayat (which came together in the Socialist Front) and the Pan Malayan Islamic Party (PMIP) whose demand is Malaya for the Malays in an Islamic theocratic state.

*   *   *

Tunku Abdul Rahman, UMNO's leader, who became his country's first Prime Minister, is a member of the royal family of the state of Kedah. He obtained a degree in history at Cambridge but he makes no claim to being an intellectual. Years of work in the Civil Service and as a District Officer helped him to get to know the people's needs at grass roots level. This, combined with what one can only call an instinct for ruling, has served him well since he went into politics.

In many respects he offers an interesting contrast to President Sukarno of Indonesia. He is not a great orator and he is certainly no dictator. As a politician he appears to work largely by intuition. He has an ease of manner and an approachability which make him a man of the people despite his princely origins.

* * *

When Malaya achieved independence in August 1957, Tunku Abdul Rahman's principal problem, and that of the Alliance government which he headed, was how to ensure that this prosperous little country could manage to exist in a world dominated by political giants. Near at hand was Communist China, with its immense population and potentialities, threatening to dominate and possibly to swallow up all South-East Asia. Malaya had already had experience of communism. The twelve-year emergency created by the communist insurrection had still not ended when the country attained its freedom from British rule. Malaya wanted no more of communism. Neither did it wish to become anybody's colony again either. But it had somehow to survive in a dangerous world and so, like other new countries, it had to rely upon outside help.

Because of its peculiar, fragmented history, it had no national army which was capable of offering any real defence against aggression. Along with independence was negotiated, therefore, a defence agreement. Under the terms of this agreement, Britain undertook to help Malaya defend its territory and accepted responsibility for training and developing the new country's armed forces. Britain was given the right to maintain units of naval, land and air forces, including a Commonwealth strategic reserve in Malaya, and thirty-year leases of land required for bases. In the event of a threatened attack against Malaya the two governments undertook to consult together and take such action as they considered necessary. If there was a threat of attack against any British territory in the East, Britain was obliged to obtain the consent of the Malayan government before committing its forces from its bases in Malaya.

No new and still developing country can feel at all secure in its continued independence without outside aid. Each, in practice, has had to turn to other, more developed countries for assistance. Indonesia, for example, has had to rely upon ever-mounting military aid from Russia. Small Malaya was clearly much more vulnerable to attack. By taking advantage of its membership of the Commonwealth it sought to solve its problems through a defence agreement which not only makes British aid available but that of other Commonwealth countries, too.

Similarly, a newly independent country must be expected to seek outside economic aid. Malaya has received economic assistance from Britain but, for the sake of its own stability and in order that it should not become anyone's stooge, it has also sought to diversify its industries, where previously its economy rested almost exclusively upon foreign-owned tin and rubber. Malaya's products go to both East and West and investment from as many directions as possible is encouraged.

The consequence of these policies has been that, despite the long years when practically everything had to be given to the fight against the communist insurrection, Malaya is today the most prosperous country in South-East Asia. Its standard of life is immensely higher than that of most of its neighbours and is in striking contrast to that of Indonesia, whose economy is in a continuous state of crisis.

The very different histories of the two countries help in part to explain the difference in standard of life—although Indonesia's natural wealth is, and has been for centuries, known to the whole world. This is Malaya's good fortune. But it is also true to say that any small country which is conspicuously better off than its larger neighbours is liable to be the object of envy and attack.

*   *   *

The territory with the most urgent problem when the idea of Malaysia was first mooted was Singapore, the little island,

26 miles long and 14 miles in breadth, joined to the Federation by a causeway only three-quarters of a mile long. Its population is overwhelmingly Chinese (1,279,000 Chinese, 238,000 Malays, 142,000 Indians and Pakistanis, 41,000 others). Life in Malaya is relatively easygoing. Singapore, situated at an international crossroads, a commercial centre with a great port, is fast-moving, pushful, aggressively dynamic. And its population is intensely politically minded.

Singapore's political life had for years been turbulent. Large sections of the Chinese had shown themselves to be sympathetic to communism and were destined, many people thought, to move further and further to the Left. Singapore had been self-governing for only a couple of years but this was already long enough to show that city-states stand little chance of survival today. The politicians in Malaya were not alone in thinking that Singapore, due to move on to independence in the near future, might soon be communist. But they had particularly good reasons for being alarmed at the prospect. Politically, economically and militarily the life of Singapore was intertwined with that of Malaya.

In the election which followed Singapore's becoming a self-governing state in June 1959, the People's Action Party, led by Mr Lee Kuan Yew, won an overwhelming majority of the votes. Before the new government could be formed, eight of the party's leaders had to be released from jail. Singapore more than made up for any lack of 'prison graduates' in neighbouring Malaya.

It was part of PAP's programme that Singapore should come to terms with the Federation and that Malay, which is the Federation's national language, should be accepted as the official language. Federation politicians tended to view with suspicion Lee Kuan Yew's talk of the need for a merger. They had no particular desire to acquire suddenly a large, predominantly Chinese, Leftist population. The absorption of Singapore into the Federation would introduce a new and disturbing political element. It would reverse the delicate

39

racial balance between Malays and Chinese. In the Federation as it stood, Malays had a slight majority. With Singapore's Chinese population inside the Federation, that Malay majority would be lost—and this in a country where Malays are the indigenous people and which retains its traditional Malay rulers and character.

Yet each needed the other. Out through Singapore went the tin and rubber upon which the Federation's economic health depended. And Singapore was Malaya's rubber market; it lived by being the Federation's shop window. 'If merger does not come with the consent of the people of the two territories,' said Lee Kuan Yew in a broadcast on September 13, 1961, 'then inevitably it will come by the use of force by one territory over the other, because each is vital to the survival of the other.'

It was in this atmosphere that the Malayan Prime Minister came up with his proposal for a Malaysia of which Singapore would be a part but which would also include the territories in northern Borneo. While these would bring with them their own quota of Chinese and, in the case of Sarawak, a fairly large Left-inclined party, the Sarawak United People's Party, their populations also included, in greater numbers, people of the same ethnic group as the Malays themselves.

Malaysia was, therefore, among other things, an obvious answer to the 'Singapore problem' from Malaya's point of view, and at the same time an answer to Singapore's own most urgent problems too. Defence, external affairs and security would be the responsibility of the central government in Kuala Lumpur, so making Singapore more secure from enemies within and without than would ever be possible if she stood on her own.

*   *   *

The problem of the three small states in northern Borneo, like that of Singapore, was how to secure independence from colonial or protected status and still survive. Until very recently Sarawak had been a quiet, peaceful little backwater, largely cut off from the world. Its history was as exotic as its people. From 1841 to 1941 it was ruled by 'White Rajahs'—Sir James Brooke, who obtained part of the present territory from the Sultan of Brunei, and his successors. Between 1941 and 1945 it was occupied by the Japanese. Then, in July 1946, Sir Vyner Brooke ceded the country to the British Crown and it became a colony.

The Government of Sarawak under the Brookes has been described as 'a benevolent despotism'. The brief period in which Sarawak was under British colonial rule was characterized by benevolence, too. This may possibly account for the fact that to this day, despite present troubles, the people of Sarawak remain some of the friendliest and most charming in the world. Crime, in the ordinary sense of the word, was almost unknown, recidivism had hardly been heard of. Life and the local administration were so far from harsh that when a prison was needed in Kuching, Sarawak's little capital, a hospital was taken over and converted to prison uses with a minimum of structural alterations. In the past the Dyaks went head-hunting from time to time, but this practice grew out of their animistic religious beliefs rather than from any natural ferocity on their part, and the last recorded raid of this sort was in 1948.

Sarawak is almost as large as Malaya itself. It is a land of exceptionally high rainfall, great forest-covered mountains and wild rivers which still provide most of its means of communication. The entire population in 1961 amounted to only 780,000. Ibans, Land Dyaks, Malays and other indigenous people (Sarawak is an anthropologist's happy hunting ground) totalled 529,000. There were 243,000 Chinese. Until recently the Ibans, or Sea Dyaks, were the largest single group but the Chinese, with a higher birth-rate, are in the process of exceeding them.

No political party existed in Sarawak in 1956 when a new constitution was granted, with a Council Negri consisting of a mixture of elected and nominated members and a Supreme Council. The day when the people of Sarawak would practise normal parliamentary democracy seemed far away. But nations today move quickly towards self-government. Three years after the granting of the new constitution the Sarawak United People's Party was formed. Its founders, Mr Ong Kee Hui and Mr Stephen Yong, had hoped that their party would be a truly national and multi-racial one. At the last moment, however, some of those they had expected to support them drew back in the belief that the time was not yet ripe for a political party, and the SUPP emerged as a predominantly Chinese party, though with some Iban support.

Although no political party as such had until then existed in Sarawak, a communist organization had been in existence ever since a number of Marxist-Leninist study groups, which had been formed in some Chinese schools in 1951, came together in late 1953 or early 1954. From this grew a communist organization which has never yet been elevated by either Moscow or Peking to the rank of 'Communist Party' but which to all intents and purposes is one none the less. From the start this organization has been clandestine.

At the time when SUPP was formed the leaders of this communist organization were looking for an opportunity for overt political activity. Within months of SUPP's formation they had moved many of their activists in all parts of the country into SUPP. And, since these were young, keen, dedicated and extremely well organized, it was not long before they had much of the local organization in their hands and, in addition, had got some of their members and sympathizers into the national leadership of the party. It has been the misfortune of the moderate SUPP leaders from that day on that much of their time and energy has had to be devoted to attempting to prevent the communist tail from wagging the democratic dog.

It was not long before half-a-dozen other parties had been formed. Of these, three were multi-racial, the other three more communal in structure. Much of this political activity and organization was a direct result of Tunku Abdul Rahman's public reference to the desirability of a Greater Malaysia which would include Sarawak. The speedy and lively reaction to the proposal, and the sudden intensification of political life to which it gave rise, grew straight out of the stage which had been reached in Sarawak's development.

Sarawak could no longer avoid being brought into the twentieth century despite the fact that large numbers of its people were still longhouse dwellers and its nomadic Punans had still to evolve any settled form of agriculture. Her little towns are predominantly Chinese and the people there were demanding more rapid social and economic development. The trouble was that Sarawak's economy, largely based on old and unproductive rubber plantations and on pepper growing, was not geared to rapid change. With colonialism fast becoming a thing of the past, the demand for self-government and independence was now being heard.

But how was a backward, slow-moving little country with a population of three-quarters of a million to achieve it? The communist organization was growing with alarming speed. How could a country with so few resources, whose political leaders were all new and inexperienced, withstand the threat from within and without? Malaysia appeared to provide the answer to many of these questions which were beginning to be asked.

*   *   *

North Borneo (Sabah) has a population composed of a polyglot collection of races. The Dusans, who are almost one-third of the population, are progressive and relatively prosperous. They have their own language, culture and music. Many of the other races are extremely primitive. The country's 475,000 population is divided between 320,000 indigenous people of one sort or another, 110,000 Chinese and 45,000 others. The country is just a little over half the size of

Sarawak. Its economy rests on timber production. Over 80 per cent of its population is engaged in agriculture.

North Borneo was a British-protected state administered by the British North Borneo Company under a royal charter since 1881; then the sovereign rights of the Company were transferred to the Crown in July 1946. The country had still to have its first elections.

After they acquired colonial status in 1946, North Borneo and Sarawak moved towards a much closer association than had been possible under the earlier régimes. By the time the Tunku made his speech in May 1961, a number of inter-territorial conferences had already been held from which had come, among other things, a Free Trade Area Agreement between the two territories. This new trend in itself reflected an awareness that if it would be difficult for an independent Sarawak to survive it would be even harder for Sabah. Each was looking for greater security and more rapid development, which would be immensely more difficult in isolation. Until the Malaysian proposal was made, independence still seemed years away for the people of both territories. Quite suddenly it became possible to envisage an early end to colonial rule.

*   *   *

There was a time when the Sultan of Brunei ruled the whole of the territories now known as Sarawak, Sabah and Brunei. But Brunei has shrunk to an area of 2,226 square miles with a population of 85,000. Of these, about 45,000 are Malays, 21,000 Chinese and the remainder indigenous. This tiny territory, one-tenth the size of Sabah, has been a British Protectorate since 1888. Its chances of being able to stand alone, one might suppose, would be small.

But Brunei has oil. Oil dominates the whole economy. It has enabled the Sultan, Sir Omar Ali Saifuddin, to carry out large-scale development projects. Brunei is the only country in Asia to have a system of old-age pensions, which, inciden-tally, is a non-contributory one. The Sultan has done well out

44

of oil, but the people of the Protectorate have benefited by it, too.

In 1959 the Sultan of Brunei promulgated the first written constitution. The existing State Council was replaced by Executive and Legislative Councils. The Sultan presides over the Executive Council, which is an appointed body. Half of the members of the Legislative Council are elected. Into the new constitution was built a safeguard: the consent of the Executive Council is required for any proposal to surrender or cede any part of Brunei or amalgamate, federate or unite any part with another territory. Supreme authority in Brunei is vested in the Sultan.

In 1961, Brunei already had a political party. This was Mr A. M. Azahari's Partai Ra'ayat Brunei (Brunei People's Party). Its object was 'a Greater Brunei, claiming all the ancient territories'.

Despite its small size, Brunei had less reason to feel the immediate need for absorption into Malaysia. Its one political party had its own expansionist aims. Uniting with a larger unit might have economic attractions for Sarawak and Sabah, but the people of Brunei could feel that some of the benefits they derived from their oil might have to be shared with others. Economically and socially they might be worse off, not better.

Yet it was unlikely that Brunei could for ever be a British Protectorate. As an independent state trying to live in isolation it would be peculiarly vulnerable. The very oil which gave the people their higher standard of life also made it a target which others, with less worthy motives than the Tunku's, might find irresistibly attractive. Malaysia, said its advocates, had something to offer Brunei, too.

The cheers which came from significant sections of the population of Singapore, Sarawak and Sabah, in response to the Malaysia proposal, were immediate and full-throated. That which came from Brunei was rather more subdued.

45

4

Prelude In West Irian

N May 1961 President Sukarno and his government had plenty to think about besides the Tunku's Malaysia plan. Their eyes at that moment were fixed, in particular, far more on West Irian than on Malaysia.

The Indonesian state which the Dutch bequeathed to Sukarno has been described as 'not a united Indonesian state but a collection of political fragments'. When the Dutch and Indonesians sat down at a round-table conference at the Hague in August 1949, transferring sovereignty from the one to the other was found to be a difficult and complex business. The United States of Indonesia was constituted as a sovereign federal republic of sixteen states, but at the last moment the signing of the agreement was delayed by the insistence of the Dutch on retaining West New Guinea (West Irian). West Irian remained Dutch—and a constant source of friction between the Netherlands and Indonesia.

In the years that followed, President Sukarno had too many problems on his hands to be able to launch any full-scale campaign to bring West Irian into the Republic of Indonesia. But it was always obvious that sooner or later this must come.

Years ago, back in the heady days of 1945, when the Japanese were soon to be driven out of Indonesia and the whole of South-East Asia, Dr Sukarno had endorsed the concept of a Greater Indonesia, to include all those territories which had been held by the Dutch and also Malaya, Singapore, the North Borneo territories and a very great deal more besides.

An Investigating Committee for the Preparation of Indonesia's Independence was established on March 1, 1945, by the Japanese military administration. On July 11, 1945, at a meeting of the Committee, Dr Sukarno outlined his hopes and plans for Indonesia:

'When I look at the islands situated between Asia and Australia and between the Pacific and the Indian Oceans,' he said, 'I understand that they are meant to form a single entity. For that reason I shall support in this meeting those who advocate that independent Indonesia should extend to Malaya and to Papua.'

* * *

With the situation in Sumatra under control after the military rebellion of 1958–61, President Sukarno was ready to turn his thoughts to the restoration of West Irian to Indonesia. The demand was a just one and it had the added advantage that it would turn his people's eyes outwards rather than inwards at a time when the economy was going from bad to worse. It was understandable that he should claim this last Dutch territory even though ethnically the link was not particularly strong. Certainly it belonged more naturally to Indonesia than to far-away Holland. This was the view of the Malayan government in Kuala Lumpur.

The question was brought up at the United Nations General Assembly. Indonesia's claim was based on the grounds that West Irian had been part of the Netherlands East Indies before 1948 and also that it had formed part of an ancient Indonesian kingdom. Various resolutions failed to get the necessary two-thirds majority and so the General Assembly failed to take any substantive action on the dispute.

The propaganda and military campaigns associated with the take-over of West Irian are worth following in some detail because of the oddly close similarity to the 'Crush Malaysia' campaign which came later.

After the failure to get a decision from the United Nations, Indonesia decided to resort to arms. All preparations were made accordingly. On December 13, 1961, President Sukarno formed a National Defence Council through which, he said, he would give his 'final commands' for the liberation of West Irian. In Djakarta on December 19 he called on all Indonesians to be ready for general mobilization with the aim of liberating West Irian and frustrating what he described as a Dutch plan to set up a 'puppet state of Papua'. This was immediately followed by the registration of both men and women volunteers. It was claimed that 100,000 had offered themselves by the end of the month. On January 3, 1962, the President proclaimed West Irian a province of Indonesia. Four days later, in a public speech, he warned that Indonesia was now ready to invade West Irian, irrespective of world opinion, unless the Dutch handed it over very quickly.

The first clash between Indonesian and Dutch forces in the West Irian area came on January 15. The Dutch claimed that an Indonesian attempt at a seaborne landing had ended disastrously for the Indonesians. The Royal Netherlands navy, they said, had successfully intercepted three Indonesian torpedo boats and now had some Indonesians as their prisoners.

An Indonesian statement issued on the following day gave an entirely different story. This said that while a unit of the Indonesian navy was making a patrol in Indonesian waters it was suddenly attacked on the open seas by units of the Dutch navy. Naval spokesmen, despite President Sukarno's statement of a few days earlier that Indonesia was ready to invade, denied that the MTB flotilla intended to invade West Irian and described the naval action as a Dutch 'provocation and act of war against Indonesia'.

In March, April, May and June 1962, small groups of Indonesian paratroopers, numbering several hundreds in all, were dropped by the Indonesian air force at a number of points in West Irian. Many of the invaders were killed, captured or dispersed in a series of isolated actions at various points along a 1,000-mile coastline. The Papuan population on several occasions gave valuable help to the Dutch forces by leading them to the scene of paratroop landings.

During this stage of the campaign, on May 8, an agreement

for the supply of further Soviet arms to Indonesia was signed in Moscow. It had already been announced by an Indonesian naval spokesman in the previous December, just as the campaign was opening, that Indonesia was buying cruisers, destroyers and submarines from a number of different countries, including the USSR, to help the liberation of West Irian as quickly as possible. The aim, he said, was to build up greater naval strength than the Netherlands.

Dutch-Indonesian talks had begun in the United States on March 20, but despite this, Indonesian paratroops landed in West Irian three days later. The negotiations were still in progress in July and August and by this time both paratroopers and marines were being used. For example, some 60 Indonesian infiltrators landed on the north coast of the Vogelkop peninsula on July 18. It was believed that they had come from bases established on the Waigeo Islands, where about 100 paratroopers had been dropped in March. On March 7–9 more than 100 marines had been landed on Misool Island, off the Vogelkop Peninsula and another 40 on the neighbouring island of Was. They were supported by Mustang fighters. The Indonesians by now were no longer denying responsibility for such landings. On the contrary, they claimed that the parachute troops who had been dropped had received considerable help from the local population.

Technically, the dispute ended on August 15 with the signing at UN headquarters of an agreement between Indonesia and the Netherlands by which administration of the territory passed to Indonesia. The campaign had brought the desired results. In a speech two days later, President Sukarno said that 2,000 volunteers had been landed in West Irian prior to the agreement. He claimed that they had established 'guerrilla pockets throughout the territory'. And he emphasized that Indonesia had no further territorial ambitions.

*　　*　　*

Response to President Sukarno's appeal for volunteers for

the West Irian campaign came not only from Indonesia. In December 1961, Ahmad Boestamam, leader of Partai Ra'ayat Malaya (PRM), the predominantly Malay Socialist Party, returned from a conference of Partai Indonesia (Partindo) in Djakarta and immediately urged the Federation of Malaya Government to give full support to the Indonesian struggle.

Mr Boestamam was a well-known Indonesiaphile, an extreme nationalist who in the past had called for bloodshed in his cause. The Alliance government was therefore not likely to wish to appear to be responding to Mr Boestamam. But its sympathies were none the less with Indonesia.

At a public rally in Kuala Lumpur on January 21, 1962, Boestamam called on Malayans to prepare to join as volunteers and struggle shoulder to shoulder with the Indonesian people to liberate West Irian.

The Labour Party of Malaya, Partai Ra'ayat's partner in the Socialist Front, assisted in organizing support for the campaign. So did various pro-Indonesian organizations. In Singapore, the small Partai Ra'ayat Singapore and the larger Barisan Sosialis did the same.

Indonesian diplomats in Singapore and the Federation openly worked to get volunteers. They concentrated their efforts in the main upon Malay nationalists, Indonesian nationals, of whom there were many in both Singapore and Malaya, and, to a lesser extent, upon extreme socialist groups. By January 1962 a West Irian Liberation Support Committee which had been formed in Singapore by Indonesian nationals had succeeded in raising 65,000 Malayan dollars for the cause. A mass rally of 2,000 people at the Consul-General's house resulted in the setting up of a West Irian Liberation Relief Committee. Even more significantly, about 5,000 youths, mostly Malays from the Malay Peninsula and Singapore, registered with the Indonesian diplomatic missions in Kuala Lumpur, Penang and Singapore. Volunteers' registration centres, operated by the Indonesian-born Welfare Association, were opened in some parts of Malaya.

Of all those who registered, only 73 were selected from the Malay Peninsula and 50 from Singapore. The campaign appeared to be as much concerned with propaganda, with building up sympathy for Indonesia and making contacts, as with the actual recruitment of volunteers. All those selected from the Peninsula were Malays of Indonesian descent or with a pro-Indonesian outlook. Nine of the Singapore volunteers were Chinese (including one girl); the remainder were Malays.

On July 4, 88 of them were entertained in Singapore by Indonesian Consulate staff. They left for Djakarta the following day in three aircraft. In Indonesia they were given commando training, including jungle fighting and parachute jumping. They were also taught sabotage techniques and intelligence procurement.

At political classes they received a course in anti-colonialism, which was given a Malaysian application. In lectures by Indonesian Army officers they were told that after their return to Malaya they should work to destroy the Alliance government by revolutionary means and that Indonesia would give them the necessary support. If this could not be achieved through an open clash it should be accomplished by subversion.

Twenty-eight of the volunteers were enrolled into an organization calling itself APREMA (Angkatan Pemuda Revolusione Malayan). This was described as a clandestine organization for the revolutionary overthrow of the Malayan government. Recruits signed an oath of loyalty in a 'Book of Blood'. Each put his signature in the book then, pricking his left thumb, sealed it with a bloody thumbprint.

As was subsequently revealed at an armed forces display in Djakarta, the Indonesians had planned a large-scale invasion of West Irian in November if Dr Subandrio's diplomacy should prove unsuccessful. In conformity with this, on August 28, thirteen days after the signing of the Indonesian-Dutch agreement to end hostilities, the Singapore volunteers were sent to

Macassar, where they were told that they were waiting to go on to West Irian. It was not until October 3 that they were brought back from this forward base to their original training camp. They were returned to Singapore on November 17 and met on arrival by Major Sardjono, Indonesian naval attaché in Singapore, and his assistant, Lieutenant Bambang Partono, who, as we shall see later, continued to play an active part among the returnees—or 'WIVRs' as they came to be known.

Most of them found great difficulty in obtaining employment and turned to the Indonesian consulate-general for assistance. A few were found jobs in trading firms with Indonesian connections. The majority lived from day to day, doing casual jobs if they were lucky. Several had married during their stay in Indonesia and were anxious to get back there again to be with their families.

As has been the case with many of the Indonesian activities in the West Irian and 'Crush Malaysia' campaigns, this episode of the West Irian volunteers looked at first sight like an exercise in melodrama or futility, or both. But in retrospect it may be seen as having been not quite so pointless after all.

* * *

The Indonesian-Dutch agreement on West Irian was signed on August 15. In a speech two days later President Sukarno denounced Malaysia as 'neo-colonialist'. The next campaign —Indonesia's 'confrontation' of Malaysia—had already begun.

5
The Theory

THE Central Committee of the PKI, on December 29, 1961, condemned Malaysia as a 'neo-colonialist plot'. This was eight months before President Sukarno publicly described it in similar terms. Both the communists and President Sukarno had already for long been talking of the 'confrontation' of the 'old-established forces' by 'the new emerging forces'. Indeed, the President has used the terms so often that these English words have become part of the language of the people. The concept owes its origins to Marxism. This does not prove that President Sukarno is a communist in disguise. What he himself has acknowledged is that he has drawn heavily upon Marxism in evolving his own philosophy and political ideology.

The concept of the confrontation of the old-established forces by the new emerging forces is of the very essence of Marx's dialectical materialism.

'All nature,' said Frederick Engels, Karl Marx's collaborator, 'from the smallest thing to the biggest, from a grain of sand to the sun, from the protista to man, is in a constant state of coming into being and going out of being, in a constant flux, in a ceaseless state of movement and change.'

Commenting on this passage, Stalin in his famous work on dialectical materialism said:

'The dialectical method regards as important primarily not that which at the given moment seems to be durable and yet is already beginning to die away, but that which is arising and developing, even though at the given moment it may appear to be not durable, for the dialectical method considers invincible only that which is arising and developing....'[1]

[1] *History of the Communist Party of the Soviet Union,* Foreign Languages Publishing House, Moscow, p. 107.

'. . . the struggle between the old and the new, between that which is dying away and that which is born, between that which is disappearing and that which is developing, constitutes the internal content of the process of development. . . .'[1]

Here is the Marxist idea of inevitable confrontation between new and old. The old is doomed to be pushed aside by that which is new; that which is new, even though it may appear weak, is none the less invincible. It is this that the communists have developed in an Indonesian context and which President Sukarno has adopted as his own.

Aidit has explained his application of this dialectical principle in these terms: 'The new emerging forces is a concept which incorporates the socialist camp, the anti-imperialist and anti-colonial newly independent countries and the progressive forces in all other countries of the world. The old-established forces incorporate the imperialist countries, colonialism and neo-colonialism as well as other reactionary forces in all parts of the world. . . . Foreign policy must be in the hands of progressives who are daring enough to oppose the criminal intrigues of the imperialists and to launch out on new paths which, however difficult or risky they may appear to be, are more beneficial to the people, to Indonesia and to the growth of the new forces that are now emerging in the world.'[2]

Aidit was commenting at the time on the situation which immediately followed the ending of the campaign to liberate West Irian. This, he said, was 'a time when the spirit of daring, the spirit of "skirting danger" was becoming a striking feature of the nationwide movement'. He went on to welcome the President's address of August 17. The Indonesian communists were embodying its ideas in what he called the 'Triple Task of the Nation'. This was (1) to consolidate the victories

[1] *History of the Communist Party of the Soviet Union*, Foreign Languages Publishing House, Moscow, p. 109.

[2] *World Marxist Review*, June 1963.

already gained; (2) to tackle the economic difficulties; and (3) to oppose neo-colonialism.

Aidit warned that today 'neo-colonialism is a very acute danger for Indonesia'. Malaysia, he said, was neo-colonialist.

* * *

As both President Sukarno and Aidit see it, their country, with its anti-colonialist record, is a natural leader of the new emergent forces against the old-established forces. Her revolution is a part of the dialectical conflict between the new and the old—but a very important part. The inference is that the Indonesian revolution will continue for so long as any régime she judges to be colonialist or neo-colonialist remains. Indonesia's rôle will be actively and militantly to campaign against such régimes, using diplomatic, military or any other means to bring them down.

Here a problem arises. The issue is relatively clear where colonies of the old type still remain, as they do in Africa. The free countries of Africa can easily pinpoint the colonies in their midst, such as the Portuguese territories of Angola and Mozambique, and they organize to assist these in their fight against colonial rule. There is no mistaking who are the old-established forces in Africa. But there are very few colonies of this type left in Indonesia's own area of the world.

But, say Sukarno and Aidit, there are 'neo-colonies'. The problem is what is a neo-colony? The old-type colony is easily identified. But it is open to the government of any country to decide who among its neighbours is a neo-colony, since there are no rules to go by. So, when Indonesia puts 'neo-colonies' among the old-established forces (because they are allegedly the puppets of the old colonial Powers) and includes them among those whom the revolution must destroy, the picture becomes disturbing. And the attempt to base foreign policies on this concept becomes potentially dangerous for any country within reach.

If, for example, Malaysia is a neo-colony because she has

Western bases on her soil and because her economy is closely bound up with that of a Western Power, does this not apply equally to the Philippines? After all, the Philippines also have immensely important Western bases on their soil; and the Philippines' economy, as every Philippine nationalist complains, is inextricably tied up with that of the United States. If the Philippines is a neo-colony, then why not Thailand, another of Indonesia's neighbours which leans heavily on the United States? The difference is only a matter of degree, and who is to decide as between one and another? If the PKI is to define who is and who is not neo-colonialist, then the net will be cast very wide indeed.

When the confrontation concept is stretched to include neo-colonies this can all too easily become a new form of imperialism, practised by one new country against another—a means by which it can impose its will upon a weaker and smaller one, make it its puppet or even annex its territory.

Once the PKI and, shortly afterwards, President Sukarno and the Indonesian government, had characterized the proposed new Malaysia as 'a neo-colonialist plot' a great deal more was bound to follow. If Malaysia was neo-colonialist then it was associated with the old-established forces and was destined to be destroyed by the new emerging ones of which the most important and, incidentally, the nearest, happened to be Indonesia.

This meant that 'confronting' Malaysia would become part of Indonesia's revolution. It gave Indonesia as good a reason for going into Malaysia as for going into West Irian. If, as most of the world had judged it to be, the West Irian campaign had been just, then, according to Indonesia's own terms, a 'Crush Malaysia' campaign would be equally just. History and the dialectical process had been on Indonesia's side when she confronted Holland in order to get West Irian. They would, according to this argument, be on her side again as she confronted Malaysia.

56

6

Rebellion

As soon as the Malaysia concept had been put forward as a practicable project things began to move quickly. Tunku Abdul Rahman publicly made the proposal, to which Indonesia gave somewhat grudging support, on May 27, 1961. In the following month Sir William Goode, Governor of North Borneo, and Sir Alexander Waddell, Governor of Sarawak, together with the UK High Commissioner in Brunei, visited Singapore to discuss the Tunku's 'Greater Malaysia' proposal with Lord Selkirk, UK Commissioner-General, South-East Asia.

Back in Kuching, Sir Alexander Waddell stated that in his view, as a preliminary to Sarawak's joining such a confederation, closer links should be established with North Borneo and Brunei. The three territories were at different stages of economic, educational and constitutional development, and not all that was involved in Malaysia could be judged until it was known how the particular interests of the three territories could be accommodated.

On July 23 a Malaysia Solidarity Consultative Committee was formed on which the various political parties in the legislatures of the five countries were represented. A month later its first meeting was held in Jesselton, Sabah.

At meetings that summer between the prime ministers of Malaya and Singapore a possible merger between the two territories in the context of the Greater Malaysia plan was discussed. It was then assumed that 'integration of the two territories' would be achieved 'in or before June 1963'.

Mr Lee Kuan Yew was publicly stressing that a merger was 'historically inevitable' and that he would be happy to see the 'Greater Malaysia' concept come about. For the moment the two ideas—of merger and the wider federation—were going forward concurrently.

From these talks between the representatives of the various territories began to emerge a more detailed idea of the form that Malaysia should take. Singapore, they agreed, would have a small number of seats in the Federal Parliament in relation to its population. In compensation it would retain control of policy relating to labour, health and education. Control of internal security would be a matter for the Central government.

On October 16 the Malayan House of Representatives approved a motion agreeing 'in principle with the concept of Malaysia comprising the eleven states of the Federation, the states of Singapore and Brunei, and the territories of North Borneo and Sarawak' and endorsing the Government's initiative.

Talks between representatives of the British and Malayan governments were held in London on November 20–22, from which came a joint statement, in the names of Mr Harold Macmillan and Tunku Abdul Rahman, announcing that they had given their approval in principle to Malaysia. Arrangements acceptable to both parties were made for the future use by Britain of the Singapore bases to assist in the defence of Malaysia, for Commonwealth defence and for the preservation of peace in South-East Asia. On the day the talks opened Dr Subandrio, as Indonesia's representative, gave Malaysia his approval at the United Nations. The practical aspects of the project were, it seemed, going ahead briskly. There appeared to be no serious obstacles in the way.

In November 1961 a Commission was appointed to visit North Borneo and Sarawak in order to ascertain the views of the peoples on the proposal. The Commission, headed by Lord Cobbold and including representatives of Britain and of the areas concerned, held hearings in North Borneo and Sarawak between mid-February and mid-April 1962. There were some 50 hearings in 35 centres. Over 4,000 people were interviewed; some spoke as individuals but most were members of delegations. Opinion there was still somewhat confused at this time. The Malaysia concept had not yet seeped down to the mass of the people. None the less, the Commission made the following assessment of the position:

'About one-third of the population in each territory strongly favours early realization of Malaysia without too much concern about terms and conditions. Another third, many of them favourable to the Malaysia project, ask, with varying degrees of emphasis, for conditions and safeguards varying in nature and extent. The warmth of support among this category would be markedly influenced by a firm expression of opinion by governments that the detailed arrangements eventually agreed upon are in the best interests of the territories. The remaining third is divided between those who insist on independence before Malaysia is considered and those who would strongly prefer to see British rule continue for some years to come.

'If the conditions and reservations which they have put forward could be substantially met, the second category referred to above would generally support the proposals. Moreover, once a firm decision was taken quite a number of the third category would be likely to abandon their opposition and decide to make the best of a doubtful job. There will remain a hard core, vocal and politically active, which will oppose Malaysia on any terms unless it is preceded by independence and self-government: this hard core might amount to near 20 per cent of the population of Sarawak and somewhat less in North Borneo.'

The Commission's belief that much of the hostility might be abandoned has been justified by events. There was undoubtedly increasing support for Malaysia as the public began to see the form it would take. As will be shown later, however, what brought the population of Malaysia together in support

59

more than anything else was Indonesia's 'Crush Malaysia' policy.

*   *   *

Mr Lee Kuan Yew had promised the people of Singapore that they would be given an opportunity to decide for themselves the type of merger they wanted. A referendum was held on September 1. In this the people were not invited to vote for or against merger but to choose the form of association with Malaysia they preferred.

Singapore politics are rarely placid. The Left-wing, communist-infiltrated Barisan Sosialis opposition—a breakaway from the PAP—in the Singapore Legislative Assembly protested that the electorate should have been given a straight 'yes' or 'no' choice. The PAP government's reply was that when the electorate voted it to power they were in fact endorsing merger, since this had been one of the planks of its election platform. It had therefore already been given its mandate. The only thing left to decide was what form of merger it should be.

The Barisan Sosialis, supported by other Left groups, responded by calling on voters to cast blank votes as a means of protesting their opposition to Malaysia. PAP replied with a Referendum Bill, which provided that blank votes should be treated as favouring the merger terms negotiated with the Federation government.

The public gave its overwhelming support to the type of merger recommended by the Singapore government—that Singapore should join Malaysia. Some 71 per cent voted for this. About 25 per cent, 140,000 people, followed the Barisan Sosialis lead and cast blank votes. The Barisan Sosialis leaders took this as a clear warning that they had already lost a lot of support in recent months and that the Malaysia project was already demonstrably weakening their position.

This local oposition from the extreme Left was predictable—after all, Malaysia was not intended to help the communists and their associates. No one supposed that four new territories could be involved in major change without some opposition, and least of all that turbulent Singapore could be brought without protest into a federation of which one of the declared purposes was to make that part of the world more safe from communism.

In December, elections were held in Sabah (at that time still British North Borneo) at which pro-Malaysia parties were returned with a majority of over 90 per cent, 95 of the 110 local council seats being won by supporters of Malaysia. Brunei had still to give its verdict on whether it believed that Malaysia would be good for it.

* * *

One day in early December 1962 a bearded man from Brunei walked into the Barisan Sosialis office in Singapore. He was thirty-four-year-old Sheikh Azahari bin Sheikh Mahmud Azahari, President of Partai Ra'ayat Brunei. Despite the similarity of names, this party bears little real resemblance to Partai Ra'ayat Singapore, or Partai Ra'ayat Malaya, both of which are Left socialist parties and within which there is a strong communist influence. Azahari was not a socialist and he was neither loved nor respected by the Barisan Sosialis leaders.

He had taken part in Indonesia's struggle against the Dutch in the late 1940s but he dreamed not of socialism but of Brunei expansionism—the uniting of the three North Borneo states into a unitary state to be known as Kalimantan Utara. He was known as a 'wild man' who loved to talk big about revolt, irresponsible and not to be taken seriously. He was a leading businessman in Brunei Town (capital of the Sultanate). The Singapore socialist leaders regarded him as corrupt. It was assumed that he was in the Indonesian government's pocket.

His party had recently won all the election seats in Brunei's Legislative Assembly, so he seemed even more irresponsible

61

than usual when he began to hint at a coming revolution and to brag that 'within forty-eight hours' he would be a prime minister. The Barisan Sosialis leaders already knew him as a braggart as well as an adventurer, so they paid little heed to what he had to say. 'The whole thing seemed futile and absurd,' one of them told me.

A few days later, on December 8, a large-scale revolt broke out in Brunei and in adjoining areas in Sabah and Sarawak. It was led by Azahari's Partai Ra'ayat. After his visit to Singapore, Azahari himself had gone to Manila, where he stayed during the revolt. From there he announced himself 'Prime Minister of the Revolutionary State of North Kalimantan'. He declared that he was prepared to fight Britain for the independence of the Borneo territories 'even if it takes twenty years'.

Groups of local Malays and Kedayans captured a number of police stations in various parts of Brunei and also Brunei Town jail, apparently in the hope of obtaining arms—shortage of which was to prove their downfall. The rebels tried to sieze the Sultan's palace, in order, it appeared, to compel him to sign a proclamation of independence for the three North Borneo territories over which the Sultan would be a constitutional monarch with Azahari as Prime Minister.

There was heavy fighting in other parts of the Sultanate and also in the affected parts of Sarawak and Sabah. The oil town of Seria, with its oil installations and airstrip, was in rebel hands for three days, as was Tutong on the coast between Seria and Brunei Town. Limbang and Lawas, Sarawak, were captured by the rebels. So, too, were the small towns of Weston and Belait, just over the border in Sabah. Rebel units numbering some hundreds threatened the important oil town of Miri, Sarawak, which is linked by pipeline with Seria.

The rebellion was virtually crushed within a few days. By December 16 all major towns in Brunei were free of rebel activities. Despite heavy fighting in several areas, there had been relatively few casualties, but hundreds of prisoners were taken. The oil installations were practically unharmed. The rebels appear to have been anxious not to make themselves unpopular by causing mass unemployment, although one of their spokesmen later expressed the view that this was a a mistake and promised that they would be destroyed 'next time'. As the fighting ended in the towns, members of the rebel army, estimated at about 1,000, took to jungle hideouts on the Brunei–Sarawak border. Mopping-up operations by Malayan and British forces had reduced the rebel army to a mere handful by the following May.

The revolt had been planned by Azahari and members of the Central Committee of his party. Azahari described those taking part in it as Tentera Nasional Kalimantan Utara (the National Army of North Kalimantan). TNKU were initials which were to acquire a wider significance in the period ahead.

* * *

Azahari remained in Manila throughout the rebellion, then flew to Djakarta in January 1963. Shortly after his arrival, Antara, the Indonesian news agency, published a list of 'cabinet members' in his 'revolutionary government'.

During the two years before the revolt, Azahari had made frequent visits to Indonesia. Almost every member of his Central Committee visited Djakarta during this same period. A year before the revolt, most of its leading members were at the Partindo Congress.

Azahari himself was in Indonesia for the last three months of 1961 and information obtained during and after the rebellion suggests that preparations for the revolt began immediately after his return to Brunei. These included the recruitment of volunteers for the TNKU who were smuggled off for training. One group of twenty left for Kalimantan (Indonesian Borneo) via Sarawak in January 1962, another of forty-six went via Sabah in April. Active in these efforts was Omar bin Alibasah, an Indonesian who took up residence in Lawas,

Sarawak, where he let it be known that he was a crocodile hunter. His 'hunting' included the recruitment of volunteers, who then posed as crocodile hunters too until there was a big enough party to be taken off secretly for military training.

Omar continued his 'crocodile hunting' for some time after the revolt, and at the time of writing is still active in the cause. Information given by Indonesian prisoners suggests that he is now busy recruiting Indonesian volunteers for the TNKU in Kalimantan.

*   *   *

On the face of it, the Brunei revolt, like the episode of the West Irian volunteers, looked like yet another exercise in futility. In fact, its consequences were far-reaching. There is no reason to suppose that most of these were not foreseen by the Indonesians, who at the least encouraged and assisted the revolt and who, the evidence suggests, more probably were directly responsible for it from start to finish. This was at first denied. Two years later, however, government spokesmen were prepared to admit its Indonesian government inspiration.[1] President Sukarno's 'Crush Malaysia' campaign may fairly be said to have started with the training of the Brunei rebels on Indonesian soil some time in mid-1962.

One immediate result of the rising which the Indonesians count as a gain was that the Sultan of Brunei was obliged to turn to the governments of Malaya and the United Kingdom for military and police assistance, as did also Sarawak and Sabah. Since the rebel remnant took to the jungle and set out to establish itself as a guerrilla army, these troops from overseas were obliged to remain there. This helped to create the image of the Borneo territories as an area which had to be held down by colonial forces. It therefore became immensely easier for propagandists to present the whole thing to the world as a 'neo-colonialist plot'.

[1] e.g. Sukarno, Indonesian Embassy press attaché, speaking at a UN Association meeting in London, November 25, 1964.

64

Moreover, the populations of the three territories got an 'introduction' to Malaya and Malayans in the shape of the Federation of Malaya's armed forces—never the best of introductions anywhere, at any time.

In addition, the Sultan of Brunei felt obliged to suspend temporarily the 1959 Constitution. The Legislative Council and District Councils were dissolved and replaced by an Emergency Council—yet another gift to propagandists eager to decry the degree of democracy so far achieved in Brunei.

Most important, Brunei decided not to join the proposed Malaysia. For six months the Sultan and his advisers had discussed with the Malayan government the terms of Bruei's entry into the enlarged Federation. The discussions broke down. The rocks on which they foundered were the disposal of Brunei's considerable oil resources and the position the Sultan should occupy among the traditional rulers of the states of the existing Federation of Malaya. It is anybody's guess whether Brunei would have stayed out of Malaysia had the revolt not occurred. The fact that she did so was Malaysia's loss. Brunei's oil would have been a useful addition to the tin and rubber which provide the basis for the economic stability of the whole group. And, of course, Brunei's population, small as it was, would have helped to achieve that racial balance which was to be a characteristic of the new Malaysia. And Brunei's future remains uncertain. Quite clearly she cannot forever stand alone.

The Brunei revolt provided the occasion for Indonesia to launch into its policy of 'confrontation' of Malaysia. On December 19, over Djakarta Radio, President Sukarno declared Indonesia's sympathy for the rebels. 'Let us march forward,' he said, 'supporting those who oppose colonialism, imperialism and oppression.' In January 1963 Dr Subandrio announced to the world that 'Indonesia must carry out a policy of confrontation towards Malaya because Malaya is now an accomplice of neo-colonialism and neo-imperialism and is pursuing an attitude of enmity towards the Indonesian people'. On February 11, the Indonesian Foreign Minister talked at a press conference of the possibility of 'physical conflict'.

On February 13, President Sukarno declared that Indonesia's opposition to Malaysia was due to his belief that Malaysia represented the forces of neo-colonialism. He warned the Malayan government that, if it persisted in its plans to form Malaysia, Indonesia would have no choice but to oppose Malaysia with political and economic confrontation.

Two days later Dr Subandrio was quoted by the official Antara agency as saying that Indonesia would give 'full assistance' to the Brunei rebels to prevent the North Kalimantan territories from entering the Malaysian Federation. It also quoted him as saying that every British troop movement in the area would be countered by one from Indonesia.

The Brunei revolt had important side-effects. Brief as it was, it provided a reason for the formation of an army of 'volunteer freedom fighters', the TNKU, into which Indonesian nationals could also later be sent as 'volunteers' and, after them, members of the regular armed forces too. Perhaps equally important, since TNKU claimed to be an army charged with the liberation of all North Kalimantan, it provided a rallying point for dissident elements in all three territories—Brunei, Sarawak and Sabah. This was of particular significance in Sarawak.

There, the Sarawak United People's Party was at that time opposing, by constitutional means, the formation of Malaysia. Its leaders argued that if Malaysia was to come it would be best for each of the three territories in North Borneo first to be given their independence and then to join Malaysia. However, when the Brunei revolt began, the SUPP leaders, in the name of their party, immediately dissociated themselves from it. They knew Azahari too well. They deplored the means he was using to achieve his ends. And his aim of a unitary state composed of the three territories, with himself in the leading rôle, had no appeal for them.

66

The SUPP, however, had within it a strong communist faction, members of the clandestine communist organization. The communists' reaction to news of the revolt was at once to acclaim it and to talk of the value of armed struggle. With parts of Sarawak adjacent to Brunei already involved in the rising, the Government on December 8 immediately introduced new security regulations empowering the Government to detain any person who appeared to be a threat to public safety. Between December 11 and 13, 50 suspected members of the communist organization were arrested under these regulations.

Following the practice in Malaya during the early days of the insurrection there, communists told younger members and sympathizers—including many Left-wingers within SUPP who had not necessarily any direct connection with the underground communist organization—that they were liable to be detained at any moment and that their best course would be to go into hiding or to escape by any means they could find. This started something of a panic rush for 'safety'. Some went into the secondary jungle or were sheltered by members of the Sarawak Farmers' Association, a peasant organization which had been set up by the communists. Several hundreds, which in time built up to something between 1,000 and 1,500, almost all of them Chinese, crossed the border into Indonesian territory.

Indonesia's record in its handling of Chinese is notoriously bad. Its treatment of its own Chinese population was well known in Sarawak and it is certain that many of the young Chinese who crossed the border in December 1962 and early in 1963 supposed that they might meet with an unfriendly reception on the other side. Instead, the first arrivals were well received. Before long they were being given training by the Indonesian Army in the art of guerrilla warfare—something which any communist would be glad to have.

The word got back that such training was available. The communist leaders were divided as to whether this was or was

67

not the moment for going over to their own armed struggle. The more experienced declared that they might have staged a rising in the first days of the Brunei revolt when Sarawak's towns had been emptied of police. But the moment had passed and the line should now be to preserve their strength for the struggle to come. Others were writing in the organization's clandestine publications of the necessity for quickly going over to the armed struggle. This encouraged still more of their members to cross the border in the hope that they, too, might be trained.

Thus even before Malaysia had become a reality Sarawak was faced with a situation where the hard core of a trained guerrilla army, composed of its own nationals, existed just over a border which was friendly to the rebels and hostile to Malaysia.

The training given to these and other dissident elements was provided by officers of the Indonesian army, but they were not enrolled into the armed forces of the Republic of Indonesia. Instead, they became members of the TNKU. This was of considerable psychological significance. Had they been made members of the regular army of a foreign and hostile power they would have been quite transparently traitors to their country and would have felt themselves to be such. The fact that they were enrolled in the TNKU made them feel like 'freedom fighters'. And they could be represented as heroes by those who were anxious to get more recruits.

Thus, within a short time after the Brunei revolt, Brunei had backed out of membership of Malaysia, Indonesia had begun its policy of confrontation and its leaders had made it clear that armed force would if necessary be used to prevent the formation of Malaysia. An armed volunteer force had been created, and was waiting on one of its borders, receiving training and assistance from the Indonesian army and pledged to the destruction of Malaysia.

Sheikh Azahari bin Sheikh Mahmud Azahari may never

have been much more than an Indonesian puppet. Omar, the crocodile hunter, may be a somewhat unorthodox recruiting officer. The Brunei revolt, which was broken in a matter of days, may not sound like one of the great successes of our time. None of these, somehow, seemed as though they need be taken too seriously. But they added up to the beginning of a campaign which in time threatened the peace of a vital area of South-East Asia.

★　　★　　★

The Brunei revolt took the Barisan Sosialis leaders in Singapore by surprise. It also confronted them with a problem. For months they had been warning their members that, since Malaysia was supposed to help to make the area safe from communism, a round-up of the extreme Left by the security authorities might be expected. Their party was particularly vulnerable because it was generally accepted that the Barisan Sosialis sheltered the island's clandestine communist organization. For their own personal reasons and for the sake of the preservation of the party itself none of them had any wish to court detention. There were divided opinions, therefore, on what should be their attitude to the revolt when their executive met for the first time after December 8.

Lim Chin Siong, the party's best known and most effective leader, who had been publicly denounced as a communist by Lee Kuan Yew, urged caution. After all, no government could be expected to take lying down the open support by its opponents of an armed rising within what would soon be the borders of its own country. A majority, however, took the line that the party must declare itself. Therefore, it had no alternative but to come out on the side of Azahari. Regardless of what they might think of the Brunei leader either as a person or as a politician, the fact was that the rising was a blow at Malaysia, to which they had already declared their opposition.

There were some who argued that there must be a forthright declaration of support in order, as one of them put it,

69

'to satisfy all the little Maos who are hopping around demanding action'. The 'little Maos' were, of course, the militant, Chinese-educated rank and file. Others reasoned that the party had always declared itself to be anti-colonial and to be on the side of those who revolted against colonialism everywhere. Azahari's aim of a North Kalimantan unitary state was certainly not their aim. The revolt was not what they would have chosen, but it still had the appearance of being anti-colonial. To remain silent would look like a betrayal of their ideals.

So from the meeting went out a declaration of support. Even as they framed it, the leaders recognized that they were preparing a noose for their own necks.

In two police sweeps in February 1963 more than 100 of the leaders and prominent United Front activists were arrested and detained. Within twelve months several of the best known of those who had been detained had already defected and publicly declared that they believed that the extreme Left now had little future in Singapore and that it must be recognized that Malaysia was coming to stay and would in due course benefit the people of Singapore.

The Barisan Sosialis Party, weakened but still very lively, continued to oppose Malaysia. But Malaysia, it seemed, was beginning to achieve, in part at least, one of its purposes even before it was officially established.

7

War In Borneo

=======

IT was not long before the 'physical conflict' threatened by Dr Subandrio had begun to materialize in other ways, too. By March, the recruiting and organizing of 'volunteers' on the West Irian pattern and their training by the Indonesian army had already started. The first incursions across the border in Sarawak began the following month, with attacks on border posts. These, according to Indonesian sources, were the work of the TNKU. This, one assumes, was intended to suggest that here was a national liberation movement, receiving the support of Indonesia, whose members were returning to their homeland as freedom fighters.

From the large number of attacks which have since been made on Sarawak and Sabah have come many prisoners. A high proportion of those captured have been regulars, some have been mercenaries engaged for this campaign, and the number of genuine volunteer 'freedom fighters' has been small indeed. Members of the first two groups in particular have talked freely.

Their stories show that all the planning, training and control is firmly in the hands of the Indonesian army. From the start those in charge of the various attacks and operations have been regular-army men. The proportion of army regulars, including company, platoon and section commanders, in the raiding parties has tended to grow as time has gone on. And the overwhelming majority are always Indonesian nationals.

By the end of 1963 about one-third of the personnel used in the operations were regulars who could not by any stretch of the imagination be classed as 'volunteers'. They were professional soldiers of the Indonesian army, sent to the territory of a neighbouring country to conduct acts of war.

The scale of those activities was indicated by figures given in a Malaysian government White Paper of October 1964. Security forces in Sabah and Sarawak recorded more than 250 incidents involving Indonesian guerrillas or aircraft between April 1963 and June 1964. In the fourteen months following the first raid of April 12, 1963, there were 158 incidents of guerrilla activities reported in Sarawak. Raids into Sabah began in October 1963, and 61 of these incidents were recorded during the course of the following nine months.

There were some sizable clashes. On October 8, 1963, for example, a party of 70 infiltrated into the Third Division of Sarawak and clashed with Malaysian security forces. During the course of the fighting 15 Indonesians were killed and 3 captured.

On another occasion, on September 26, 1963, a force of over 60 men, organized in three platoons, entered Sarawak and began an attack on Serikin in the First Division.

Three days later, a force of at least 90 attacked Long Jawi in the Third Division. And, in the Fourth Division on the same day, a group of 60 men was contacted by the security forces at Bukit Biru.

On March 6, 1964, a whole platoon of the Indonesian army's 328 Raider Battalion (a 'crack' Indonesian unit which had served in the Congo) was located by security forces on the northern slopes of Klinkang Range in Sarawak. This platoon was made up entirely of soldiers of the TNI—the Indonesian regular army.

We are not here so much concerned with a detailed record of events, or with a history of Indonesia's confrontation of Malaysia, as with the background to confrontation, its roots, form and consequences. What does need to be appreciated, however, is that behind the statistics lies the virtual dislocation of Malaysia's normal life, a blow aimed at a new nation's economy, a curb put on the development of a country which was already making exceptional progress and is anxious and able to give its people a steadily rising standard of life. And behind these, again, is a great deal of human tragedy.

First there are the people at the receiving end. The Dyaks, or Ibans, living their simple lives in the longhouse villages —and people of much more primitive races, too—now go in constant fear of raids from across a border of which in the past they were hardly conscious. They know little of encirclement, neo-colonialism, confrontation or the designs of ambitious politicians. They cannot comprehend the predatory dreams of governments determined to be recognized as 'great' and 'powerful'. They only know that their homes are destroyed, their people killed by men whom they have supposed to be their brothers and who now inexplicably come to them with fire and sword.

The bewilderment of some of these unsophisticated border Dyaks has sometimes turned to fury. Even while Indonesian radio propagandists were telling their public that the Ibans welcomed the Indonesians as deliverers, those same Ibans, in an outburst of spontaneous indignation, were giving the intruders a far fiercer reception than they would ever get from the uniformed security forces.

The Indonesian army regulars who have played an increasingly important part in confrontation are just doing a job. It is one for which most of them have little taste. They were brought up to see the people of Malaya, Sarawak and Sabah as their brothers. What is now Malaysia was seen as friendly territory. There were bonds of blood, religion, culture and language.

Yet they now found themselves involved in a war which could give no joy to any regular soldier who had a pride in his profession. It was a furtive, mean little hit-and-run affair. As likely as not, the professional knows that he will be described in any communiqués as a 'volunteer', an amateur. And more often than not when he goes into action there will be a good proportion of such amateurs in his group—poorly trained men who in action may prove to be as much a liability as an asset. Added to this there may also be a small sprinkling of Sarawak and Malayan Chinese communists. He has been taught by his

3*

government, and by his government's policies, to view the Chinese with suspicion. As a soldier he probably has little love for communists either. It may even be that in the past he has been in action against members of the PKI, so that they are identified in his mind with the enemy of earlier campaigns.

The regulars are in the main puzzled, sometimes resentful, and strongly suspicious that this is no cause for which to die. The Indonesian government clearly recognizes this. Most of the regulars who have been taken prisoner have reported that they were not told until their final briefing that they were to be used against Malaysia. Then, at the very last moment before going into action, they were told that they were off to Malaysia, there to try to establish jungle bases as a preliminary to guerrilla war. Until then they were given the impression that they were on their way to a training exercise.

One cannot help feeling some compassion for the Indonesian 'volunteers' who normally make up perhaps one-third of any given group of intruders. Indonesian propaganda claims that these men are demanding in their millions to be sent to join the freedom fighters in the glorious struggle to liberate Malaysia from the neo-colonialist yoke. But usually there is nothing very glorious about them, just as in practice there is nothing glorious about the struggle in which they are engaged.

There are smugglers (and this is an area where smuggling has for long been a major industry) who have been caught by marine police patrols and offered the choice of jail or the 'volunteers'. There are men newly out of prison who have been press-ganged into the TNKU. Others, bewildered, simple-minded, rather pathetic creatures, who have been put under pressure by their village headmen (who likewise have been pressed by government agents to provide a quota of volunteers). And there are the small minority who see the attempt to crush Malaysia as part of Indonesia's great revolution, a continuation of the old, proud struggle against those who would destroy Indonesia and enslave her people—'the

74

old-established forces'—the Western Powers, who did it before and are trying to do it again.

The volunteers, in particular, talk freely. They are not disciplined soldiers; neither, in most cases, have they any cause to which they feel a deep loyalty which might lead them to remain silent. From the vast mass of case histories which now exist in the Malaysian government's records one could select dozens of every type, but here is a more or less random selection.

Badut bin Sukop was at one time a jungle fighter in Celebes, which is his home. He was in action against the Tentera Nasional Indonesia—the Indonesian Army. Then he became a barter trader. ('Barter trading,' so far as Indonesia is concerned, means smuggling.) Thus he was vulnerable on two counts, as a former rebel and as a present smuggler. In June 1963 he was arrested as a smuggler by an officer of the Korps Komando Operasi, the Indonesian marines. Badut was told that he could either join the KKO or he would find himself in prison for six months on a smuggling charge. He opted for the KKO and joined a group of about 100 strong. His morale was already low before his capture, because a party from his own group of trainees which had previously gone across the border had left ten of their number behind, buried in the jungle.

Marimin bin Arjo is a forty-year-old Javanese, a small farmer. He served in the Dutch Army for three years, fought the Japanese during the war and was imprisoned by them. His military experience attracted the attention of those who were trying to recruit 'volunteers'. He was approached by an Army sergeant but refused to join. Then he was told that if he would not enlist for Sabah the next day he would go to jail. So Marimin went off at night into Sabah, in a party led by Omar the crocodile hunter.

Alimas bin Lady was particularly susceptible to pressure. He had been out of jail for just a month, after serving a three-year sentence, when he was pressed to join a group of 'volunteers' who were undergoing training in Nunukan. After one month's training he was sent with a group into Sabah where, in deep jungle, they lost their way. He managed to break from the main party and wandered about on his own for a time, having decided to give himself up to the security forces, as in due course he did.

Patabaki, otherwise known as Yunus bin Pesau, an impoverished small farmer, was given only five days' military training after he had been pressed into joining by a member of the KKO. Like Alimas bin Lady, he and his party lost their way in Sabah. He surrendered after days of wandering in a mangrove swamp. He and his detachment had been without food for about twenty days. They managed to survive by eating young leaves and sea snails.

From the bare facts, given in cold, official language, a picture is built up of men who in the main have never known anything but poverty and hardship and who are treated as expendable by those responsible for the confrontation campaign. They present, individually and collectively, a picture very different from that offered to the world by their government's propagandists. Their names, to the Westerner at least, may seem romantic, the terrain in which they operate may sound exotic. But there is nothing romantic or exotic for the volunteers about the experiences they have had.

Then there are the other young men, and women too, who take part in these raids. Mostly they are the fodder of confrontation even though they went to Indonesia to learn the art of guerrilla war so that they might use it for their own cause of communism.

I recall being present in an operations room when a report was received over the telephone which told of the latest raid into Sarawak. The raiders had been ordered to attack a military encampment in which there was a strong concentration of first-rate fighting men with everything in the way of modern weapons and equipment required for dealing with very much larger groups of intruders than this. The same sort of raid had been attempted a few days earlier on the same target. The intruders had been repulsed with fairly high losses in dead and wounded.

This time they came at night. But darkness was no real cover, for the security forces had been alerted by the previous raid, in which they had had their losses, too. One would have thought that those who had sent these men across the border would have known what their reception was likely to be. The security forces opened fire; the raiders beat a hurried retreat. They left behind the best part of a dozen dead. These included Indonesian 'volunteers', ill-prepared for such activities, and a Sarawak Chinese boy of perhaps twenty years of age, still wearing his SUPP badge—he had been a member of the clandestine communist organization within the party.

As the man who took the call from the jungle put down the receiver he said, more to himself than to me, 'They just don't stand a cat in hell's chance. It's the sheer, cynical inhumanity of those who send them here that makes me fighting mad.'

*　　*　　*

For the men on the other side who must try to stop the intruders before they establish Indonesian bases on Malaysian soil, there is nothing to recommend confrontation.

Northern Borneo is an area of jagged mountains, vast unexplored jungles, wild rivers and huge swamps. The rainfall is almost the highest in the world. Jungles and swamps steam eternally in the tropical heat. It is primordial country. This means that in some respects it is good guerrilla country. But it is immensely hard on intruders and defenders alike.

The point of entry into Sabah is most frequently through a maze of rivers and mangrove swamp. The intruders come by boat and may as likely lose themselves in swamp as in deep jungle. In Sarawak, they may come through the jungle or over immensely steep, jungle-covered mountains.

The defenders are Malaysian, British and Gurkha soldiers. Between them, in less than two years from the time the Indonesian raids began, they killed or captured, to their knowledge, some 3,000 intruders, most of them in ambushes, in small skirmishes or in chance encounters when they were out on patrol. How many dead the intruders dragged back with them over the border or left to rot in the jungle may never be known to either side.

Most of the activity is in deep jungle—and Borneo's is some of the 'deepest' on earth. No one who has not experienced it can imagine what life there is like. Millions of 100-feet forest giants are packed so close together, stretching for hundreds of miles, that their topmost branches form an unbroken, incessantly dripping cover through which no daylight penetrates. Under them men must read by candlelight at full noon. The parasitic creepers which hang down from the great trees are joined by upward-pushing undergrowth.

Through such often viciously barbed undergrowth men hack their way, making perhaps less than one mile's progress in a couple of days. Intruders found within 1,000 yards of the border may have travelled miles, cutting their way along winding jungle tracks and taking ten days to get there. The defenders may hear them near at hand, yet be separated from them by hours of exhausting 'jungle bashing'.

For the British troops in the Borneo jungle this is as hard an assignment as they are likely to find anywhere. They were brought in at the request of the Malaysian government, in accordance with the Malaysian–British defence agreements. They would leave tomorrow with the greatest joy. They have no cause to love confrontation.

*   *   *

While Indonesia was quietly building up what gradually came to be recognized as a serious military effort aimed at killing the new Federation before it was born, things were moving forward at the democratic level in the territories concerned.

In June 1963 Sarawak held its second elections. Sarawak

has universal suffrage and a rather confusing indirect, three-tier system. Of the 429 seats contested, 313 were won by candidates supporting the Malaysia project and 116 by candidates opposed to it. This is something of a simplification, both as to the distribution of support and the issue of Malaysia itself.

Broadly speaking, support for the parties follows racial lines. A breakdown of the figures shows that SUPP, which has been described as 'anti-Malaysia', got the support of the majority of the Chinese; the great majority of Ibans voted for the 'pro-Malaysia' Alliance, which came to victory mainly on their support. The two main racial groups are almost evenly balanced. The Chinese accounted at that time for 31·5 of the population, the Ibans for 31·11 (by now the Chinese have a slight edge over the Ibans, since their numbers are growing more quickly).

But to describe the SUPP vote as solidly anti-Malaysia is also an over-simplification. It was, for many people, first and foremost a pro-Chinese vote—for the party's two principal leaders are leading figures in the Chinese community. Moreover, while SUPP was opposing Malaysia in its proposed form, it was not hostile to the Malaysia concept as such. When, in fact, Malaysia became a reality, SUPP accepted it. Indonesia's military activities against Sarawak finally brought the leaders out against confrontation and for the defence of Sarawak against Indonesian aggression. It goes almost without saying that the possibility of Sarawak's joining Indonesia or becoming part of the sort of North Borneo unitary state which Azahari stood for was never raised as a serious issue in the election.

Elections had already been held in Sabah in December 1962. There the supporters of Malaysia had an overwhelming victory, winning 95 of the 110 seats.

The Malaysia whose formation Indonesia was trying to prevent was not, apparently, seen as a neo-colonialist plot by a majority of those whose lives it touched most closely.

8

Psywar Diplomacy

SIDE by side with Indonesia's military confrontation of Malaysia went a diplomatic one, too. To Indonesia, confrontation is not just a policy dreamed up for the purpose of imposing her will upon Malaysia. It is at the very root of what Dr Sukarno and his colleagues regard as their own distinctive ideology but which they urge other Afro-Asian countries to accept.

The cornerstone of this, as we have noted, is the fundamentally Marxist concept of the inevitable confrontation of the old-established forces by the new emerging ones. Upon this Indonesia's leaders base their foreign policies. As a consequence, they reject the old, accepted approach to international relations. They come to the conference table with a new one which derives from their own belief that this is, as President Sukarno has called it, 'the era of confrontation'.

Their diplomacy is therefore a diplomacy of confrontation and as such a part of Indonesia's attempt to ensure that the emergent forces shall prevail over the old and those who go along with them.

From the time that Malaysia was first advanced as a practical proposition there have been meetings between Malaysian and Indonesian leaders. Dato Dr Ismail told the Security Council that there had been 'at least ten' of these. During 1963 such meetings came in quick succession. In Tokyo on May 31 Prime Minister Tunku Abdul Rahman discussed Indonesia's confrontation policy with President Sukarno. It was agreed that there should be a return to the spirit of the Malayan-Indonesian Treaty of Friendship and an end to acrimony.

A week later, on June 7, the Malayan Deputy Prime

Minister, Tun Abdul Razak, Dr Subandrio of Indonesia and Signor Emanuel Pelaez of the Philippines, met at a Foreign Ministers' Conference in Manila. The Indonesian and the Philippine Foreign Ministers declared their wish to welcome the establishment of Malaysia after the Secretary-General of UN or his representative had been able to ascertain that the peoples of Sabah and Sarawak were in favour of joining Malaysia.

On July 30 there was another conference in Manila, this time a 'summit' of the heads of government of the three countries. President Sukarno, President Macapagal and Tunku Abdul Rahman endorsed the Foreign Ministers' recommendations. Tunku Abdul Rahman stated that the people of Sarawak and Sabah had already made clear at the polls their support for Malaysia, and he and the British government had long ago announced August 31 as Malaysia Day, the day on which colonial rule would come to an end in Singapore and the Borneo territories. Despite this he accepted the suggestion that a United Nations team should satisfy itself that the elections had truly expressed the views of the people. He also agreed that Malaysia Day would, if necessary, be postponed.

The three leaders endorsed a Philippine proposal that they should take initial steps towards the establishment of some sort of loose federation of their three countries, to be known as Maphilindo. It seemed reasonable to assume that this was the expression of a hope for the future rather than a piece of immediate practical politics. Apart from anything else, Indonesia has ten times Malaysia's, and more than three times the Philippines', population and so would completely dominate them if such a federation was formed. Added to this is the fact that Indonesia has the largest communist party in the non-communist world. Until events have shown whether Indonesia's future is with the PKI or with the non-communists it is unlikely that either anti-communist Malaya or the equally anti-communist Philippines could be happy as junior partners inside Maphilindo.

At no time did there appear to be much evidence that these conferences, and others which were to come later in Bangkok and Tokyo, were intended by the Indonesians to bring confrontation to an end. The various diplomatic moves of this period looked more like working demonstrations of 'confrontation diplomacy'.

President Sukarno's propaganda machine has for years worked hard to popularize the idea of 'Malay unity' and 'unity of all Malay races'. President Sukarno has been built up in his own country as the leader of 'all the Malays', and he is presented in this way to the peoples of the Philippines and Malaysia—both of whom come into the category of 'Malay races'. Indonesian leaders have from time to time talked of a return to the ancient Indonesian empire. But the 'Malay unity' line is one which is of greater significance; understandably it gets a response from among certain sections of the Malayans and Filipinos, and for this reason should be taken more seriously. Maphilindo is a new word for an old idea.

The Maphilindo proposal, like so much else, has now been made a weapon in Indonesia's psywar with Malaysia.

*   *   *

There was an atmosphere of unreality in Kuching when the United Nations team of investigators, requested by the Manila Conference and sent to Sarawak and Sabah by U Thant, arrived on August 16. No one on the spot could doubt for one moment that these UN officials could do anything other than confirm what everyone already knew, and which the Opposition leaders themselves were prepared to admit, namely that the elections had broadly reflected the will of the people. Equally, no one supposed that Indonesia would accept the findings should they prove favourable to Malaysia. The team split up into two groups, one remaining in Sarawak and the other going on to Sabah. Anyone who knew anything about the situation at all watched with sympathy these serious-minded, intelligent members of Western, communist and 'new' countries conscientiously doing their job, accompanied by a large group of official Indonesian, Philippine and Malayan observers.

The expected happened. The team reported, as the facts of the case obliged it to do, that the elections had shown that a majority of the people supported pro-Malaysian candidates. And, as was also expected, the Indonesians did not permit their policy of confrontation to be diverted for one moment either by the presence of the UN team or by its findings. The raids continued.

Malaysia Day had been put off from August 31 to September 16. This reflected the Tunku's anxiety to reach accord with Indonesia, for the postponement conflicted with an agreement reached between Malaya and Britain and was accepted by him despite the fact that this also directly concerned the governments of Sabah, Sarawak and Singapore, all of which immediately protested at the delay.

The Indonesians for their part protested that Malaysia Day should have been further postponed until after the UN Secretary-General had pronounced his judgment. This incident, they were to say later, convinced them that Malaysia must be crushed. In fact the 'Crush Malaysia' campaign was already many months old, which was precisely why the UN observers were there at all.

There was an air of even greater unreality when, in June 1964, President Sukarno agreed to withdraw Indonesian guerrillas from Sabah and Sarawak so that yet one more summit, this time in Tokyo, might begin. Thailand sent teams of observers to verify the withdrawal. Neither they nor anyone else was able to explain just how this could be done when guerrilla bands had for months been coming across an unmarked border stretching for 1,000 miles over tops of mountains and through some of the densest jungle on earth. But Thais do not normally permit themselves to be weighed down unduly by life's problems. Their government had agreed to set up two checkpoints, one in Sabah, the other in Sarawak, and this the members of the teams tried to do. A party of them set off on June 18 for Tebedu, three miles from the Sarawak–Indonesia border.

Predictably, a party of thirty-two Indonesian 'irregulars' on that same day encountered a security patrol five kilometres from the border. They were conducted to the checkpoint, explaining as they went that they had been in the jungle for some time. They were bronzed, fit but tired. It was observed that, remembering the inhospitable nature of the jungle 'floor', their feet were in surprisingly good shape. It was all a little too good to be true and subsequent investigations showed fairly conclusively that these 'irregulars' had been specially sent across the border so that they might at the right moment 'withdraw' and so create the impression that Indonesia was adhering to the terms of the agreement.

The summit talks ended abruptly in Tokyo; the Thai observers almost as abruptly returned to Thailand in no way surprised, one suspected, by the unsatisfactory outcome of the operation. Almost within hours of the ending of the talks in Tokyo, yet one more armed raid into Sarawak was staged, with the usual clash with the security forces—and the usual casualties.

*   *   *

During the summit meeting, President Macapagal put forward a proposal that the dispute should be submitted to a four-nation Afro-Asian conciliation commission. President Sukarno took up the suggestion. The Tunku, suspecting that the Indonesians were more concerned with propaganda than with peace, said that he would accept it only if Indonesia stopped its confrontation of Malaysia and withdrew its guerillas from Sabah and Sarawak. The proposal came to nothing.

When, as in this case, psywar takes priority over all else, every move, every word by those who conduct it, is inevitably made suspect.

9

The Terrorists

TOWARDS the end of 1963 Malaysian press and public began to talk of the 'mad bomber of Singapore'. A maniac with an interest in explosives was, it seemed, at large in Singapore. Sticky-bombs were thrown at cars in a car park. Two Indian passers-by were killed. The mad bomber, operating at night, even threw explosives of some sort at benches and trees in a public park. Then the story began to go around that this was not the work of an escaped lunatic armed with a supply of TNT, hand-grenades and sticky-bombs, but all part of Indonesia's campaign against Malaysia. There must have been many people besides myself who thought that this was far-fetched. It looked like a naïve attempt by the Malaysian government to 'blame everything on the Indonesians', but which would simply have the effect of bringing the government itself into disrepute.

Gradually, however, it became apparent that the mad bomber might not be so mad after all. In the first place, there was an increasing number of the sort of incidents which had been attributed to him. They soon added up to too many for any one individual. Secondly, the targets became increasingly military. Trees in a public park were one thing, hotels and domestic property were border-line cases, telephone booths and then bridges were quite another. Before long it was quite obvious that the incidents were the work of an organized group or groups.

This did not prove that such groups were Indonesian-inspired, and to label them in that way might still be just so much war propaganda. Then some of the terrorists were caught and before long there was plenty of evidence to show who and what they were and what was their inspiration.

They were an oddly assorted group, but with certain things in common. All had been trained in terrorism on Indonesian soil by the Indonesian army, then provided with the materials and equipment required for conducting acts of sabotage. They had also been provided with the necessary transport to get them back to Singapore and, in most cases, a fairly generous supply of Malaysian dollars to keep them going. The majority were, it was revealed, Malaysians who had been recruited by Indonesia for use against their own country.

There were non-political, misguided mercenaries, recruited from among the unemployed and discontented. In most cases these were very low-grade human material, the sort of men who either because of lack of intelligence, political background or integrity could be bought by pretty well anyone. They were described by those who questioned them—and found them very ready to talk—as 'riff-raff'. From the Indonesian point of view, these were obviously the expendables. And the Indonesians threw them away quite heartlessly.

But after the riff-raff came members of little conspiratorial, extremist nationalist groups—Malays, or Malaysians of Indonesian origin. These stood for something although, it usually transpired, not for very much. They were still not rated high as human material, but they were slightly superior to the first category. Among them were a score of WIVs, trained for, though not used in, the West Irian campaign. The West Irian Liberation Support Committee also provided some recruits.

After these came members and, surprisingly, sometimes even publicly known leaders, of overt Malay nationalist groups and parties of the extreme Right. And after these again people at the other end of the political spectrum, dedicated young Chinese members of organizations of the extreme Left like Partai Ra'ayat Singapore and communist sympathizers within the orthodox Labour movement. Later events on the Malay Peninsula showed that this was what must be regarded as the normal pattern of this aspect of confrontation—the use of human material which is very low-grade indeed at the start of a particular campaign, and then a gradual improvement until in time a very tough, dedicated type of personnel is used.

Much that a year earlier had seemed inexplicable now became clear: the Indonesians' recruitment of volunteers for the West Irian campaign; the enrolment of some of them into curious little conspiratorial, oath-taking groups; and the training of volunteers in terrorism and sabotage as well as guerrilla warfare. All this began to take on significance as the campaign in Singapore built up. For example, among some of the more active and better-trained terrorists who fell into the hands of the police were WIVs. Their training in terrorism might never have had much place in the West Irian campaign, but it was being put to use now in Singapore.

In time it was established that several score of Malaysian nationals from Singapore and the Peninsula had received training in sabotage at various bases in Indonesia. The training included guerrilla warfare, handling of small arms and sabotage. The brighter ones among them were also given political indoctrination and courses in intelligence procurement and in personal security.

One group brought with them to Singapore a quantity of arms, grenades, ammunition and explosives, most of which fell into the hands of the police shortly after they were landed. Another group of saboteurs was accompanied by Indonesians. These brought with them Sten guns, pistols, ammunition and explosives, which were in due course recovered by the security authorities.

The arms and explosives usually arrived in vessels used by barter traders and were concealed in sacks of charcoal or under cargoes of copra. On their return to Singapore, the trained saboteurs were expected to destroy oil refineries, military installations and public utilities such as power stations, bridges and water pipelines.

They had also been instructed that, should they fail to reach their assigned targets, they should use their explosives at random. Which helped, of course, to explain the strange behaviour of the 'mad bomber'.

At the UN Security Council Meeting, Dr Sudjarwo was to say later: "I am proud that my people, especially our revolutionary youth, are prepared to sacrifice so much to risk their lives in the cause of freedom, in the fight against colonialism and neo-colonialism.' A look at the case-histories of a few of the individual types Indonesia did in fact use may be instructive if only because they have their opposite numbers in practically any recently independent, developing country today.

*　　*　　*

Nordin bin Lemon was a 'non-political' who led one of the groups whose activities helped to create the legend of the 'mad bomber'. His story is a very human one. Born in 1937 in Malacca, he was educated up to standard two. His formal education ended in 1946 when he was still only nine years of age, and he has always yearned for more education. His mother died when he was five and as a consequence he was passed to his grandmother, then back to his father, a local-born Indonesian who by then had remarried. At the age of eleven he quarrelled with his stepmother and ran away from home. He survived by working as dishwasher, laundryman and for a time helping his grandfather, who was a dealer in buffaloes.

Fame and fortune, both on a limited scale, came to Nordin bin Lemon when he became known to the public as 'Tiger Lemon', professional boxer. It was during this brief period of relative affluence that he met his future wife in a hotel where he was staying. Her stepfather was a vice-consul at the Indonesian consulate; her mother, first wife in a polygamous marriage, left her husband when a second wife was brought in. In due course the mother obtained a divorce and went off to Djakarta, taking with her her daughter, who by now was Nordin's wife. By this time Nordin was no longer famous; his boxing career was finished.

When his wife left him in 1961 she took their daughter with her. Nordin tried to dissuade her but without success. He did not see his wife again until he went to Djakarta as a West Irian volunteer. A friend had told him that a way of getting to Indonesia would be to register with the Indonesian consulate as a volunteer. 'My only reason for going,' he says, 'was to take the opportunity to see my wife and child.'

In Indonesia he was the only one of his group who understood the Indonesian dialect. As an ex-boxer, he was good at foot-drill. So they made him a platoon commander. The WIVs were disbanded. Nordin was sent home to Singapore. His hope was that he might be able to get a job, earn some money, then return to his wife. But like other WIVs he found it difficult to get work, spent much of his time unemployed, and so found it impossible to save. 'I began to get desperate,' he says, 'so I went to the Indonesian consulate and asked for help.' This was in April 1963. By this time the assistant naval attaché, Bambang Partono, was busy preparing the way for the terror campaign in Singapore which Indonesia was already planning. In almost every captured terrorist's story the name of Bambang Partono appears.

Bambang had plenty of jobs for a man like Nordin to do. He asked him to contact other returned WIVs with families in Indonesia. When Nordin had collected five he was instructed to take them to a jetty at a Singapore shipbuilding yard where an Indonesian torpedo boat was undergoing repairs. Nordin took the recruits along and handed them over to the Captain, who promised to take them to Indonesia. Nordin bin Lemon felt that he was doing useful work at last, helping men to join their families with free passage provided by the Indonesian government. And he was a 'somebody' again.

A grateful Indonesian government gave him 800 dollars so that he might set up a little coffee-stall of his own. He used half of this sum to buy clothes as presents for his wife; with the other half he bought a coffee-stall. But it was not the

Indonesian intention just to set him up as a small business-man. His coffee-stall was made the contact place for volunteers who were sent to him and whom he was expected to direct to Indonesian marine police boats.

In time he got to Indonesia again, taking with him gifts for his wife. But he was made leader of a group of WIVs and other Malays who were already assembled there. Along with the others he was taught the use of explosives and the technique of sabotage. He was made camp commandant. And all the time he was asking to be allowed to get to his wife in far-away Djakarta and being given reasons why it was impossible to go just yet. 'No one mentioned,' he says, 'that our training would be for use in Singapore.' He was able briefly to see his wife in Djakarta, then in December he was told that he must go back to Singapore to put his training into practice. He was given a supply of explosives and a map and put in charge of a small group of terrorists. A look at the map showed him the nature of the operation: they would be expected to blow up a pipeline or a railway track. They appear to have disposed of their explosives indiscriminately and helped to create the legend of the 'mad bomber of Singapore'.

In due course he learned from his wife of the birth of a son. 'If I am freed,' he said, 'I will write and ask her to come to me in Singapore with our children. If she will not come, then I will not go back to Indonesia and I must learn to forget all about them.' Nordin bin Lemon is officially described as 'an intelligent, friendly man'.

Kassim bin Ahmad might be classified as a 'low-grade political'. Indonesian-born, he came to Singapore in 1943. Four years later he was already involved in extremist Malay nationalist activities. After this he went into Partai Ra'ayat Singapore, which was formed by Malay extremists who were also socialists. Kassim bin Ahmad was anti-Chinese and it was his anti-Chinese prejudices which the Indonesians were able to exploit. He in turn worked upon the racial feelings of Malays he knew, in order to win them as recruits. By going to Indonesia, he told them, they would be able to help to save Malaya from falling into Chinese hands—but, for this, military training would be required.

One night twenty men recruited by Kassim and others set out, under cover of darkness, in two boats, both stolen. In Medan, Indonesia, they were trained in fixed-bayonet fighting, intelligence procurement, map and compass reading, the techniques of psychological warfare, sabotage, espionage. They were taught the use of hand-grenades and explosives as used on buildings, railway lines, bridges, power stations. They were instructed also in the silent killing of guards, sentries and others, 'with or without knives'.

Kassim was provided with ample cash. On one occasion he returned with 15,000 dollars in his possession. When he wanted more he asked in letters for '200 mats for use in a newly completed mosque'. One 'mat' equalled 1,000 dollars. But the Indonesians, though willing to pay him generously, were not prepared to be as generous as that. Kassim was made a lieutenant-colonel in the Tentera Nasional Republic Malaya, the militant arm of the Peninsula Malay Union.

Members of Partai Ra'ayat Singapore who went into similar secret work have told how they were made to swear on the Koran an oath calling upon Allah to curse them should they betray the organization. As with APREMA, formed among the WIVs in Indonesia, the oath was signed and sealed with their blood.

Kahar bin Hamid, otherwise known as Bong Kahar, was at one time a dog-shooter in Singapore. But he was also a big man in his own little political world of Malay extremism. Bong Kahar was President of the Singapore Peninsula Malay Union, Vice-President of the PMU Malaya and leader of the PMU Youth Section. In March 1963 he met Lieutenant Bambang Partono along with seven West Irian volunteers. Bong Kahar was just the sort of man Lieutenant Partono wanted to meet. The Peninsula Malay Union was against Malaysia. It also lacked funds. So the man who had previously earned a living by shooting stray dogs was given a first payment of 25,000 dollars in cash to put the PMU on its feet. In return Bong Kahar would find recruits to go to Indonesia. Members of his party would also find landing points for submarines and suitable places, such as open fields and hillsides, for use as dropping zones for Indonesian planes which, at the appropriate time, would bring arms and paratroops.

With some of the cash he had been given, and from subsequent gifts which brought the total up to 36,000 dollars, he bought typewriters, office equipment, a duplicator, a microphone and a Morris Minor van for the party. But much of it he gave away—1,000 and 1,500 dollars at a time—to nine of his political associates who happened to be in debt. The stories of a number of detainees and prisoners include similar details reflecting their 'easy come, easy go' attitude towards the large sums of cash they received. Sometimes it was given away; quite frequently as much as 1,000 dollars was spent on jewellery and clothing for their wives. Rarely was more than half of the initial sum used for its intended political purposes.

Raslan Sharif, a cap-maker of Sumatran origin, was also well known in his own political world, this time that of the extreme Left. Raslan Sharif was secretary of the Johore Division of Partai Ra'ayat; secretary of the Malayan Peoples' Socialist Front, Johore Division; chief publicity officer of Partai Ra'ayat Malaya; and also the party's candidate in Johore Bahru town elections in April 1961. Using a connection he already had with Partai Indonesia, he succeeded in persuading the party's national leaders that he should go to Indonesia for political training. While he was there he attended a political cadres course and also helped to form APREMA among Partai Ra'ayat members who were already there as WIVs.

Two years later he was back in Indonesia again, this time for training in the techniques of guerrilla warfare. He returned to Singapore along with a party of others. They brought with them a cargo of explosives. He then set about establishing courier links, mainly contacts among fishermen, and organizing transport of men and materials from Indonesia. He was arrested while engaged in this on March 10, 1964.

*　　*　　*

It seems likely that many who were recruited by Raslan Sharif, Bong Kahar and the others did not fully realize that they were going to be used by Indonesia for purely Indonesian purposes. Most appear to have been ignorant of the overall confrontation plan. They believed that they were assisting the revolution, which was the aim of the small extremist organizations to which they belonged. In some cases this was to be a Malay nationalist revolution which might be described as of the extreme Right, in others a socialist revolution of the extreme Left. Frequently both Malay nationalism and socialism are combined in the one individual.

For the Malay nationalists the Indonesians initiated the formation of a 'revolutionary government', known as Negara Republic Malaya, with the TNM as its 'national army'. This was better organized than APREMA, which it replaced. Both the 'government' and its 'army' were active in Singapore and the Malayan Peninsula, but had their headquarters in Tanjong Balai in Indonesia.

It was all conceived in the most grandiose way. The TNM was given a proper command structure. Paper zones of command in Singapore and the Peninsula were established and zone commanders nominated. TNM groups were to be fortified with regular Indonesian army personnel. The first recruits were taken across to Indonesia in February 1964. They were mostly of low calibre and it is doubtful whether more than a small proportion were able to absorb the training they were given. It is certain that the Indonesians threw them into action too soon. Men of rather higher calibre began to come when recruitment was started among organized political groups.

In none of the many organizations used or specially created

93

were the numbers of members large. But the Indonesians showed themselves willing to use anyone, no matter how crackpot they or their organizations might be, provided they were prepared to be trained and supplied with explosives. The Indonesians appear to have been completely cynical both in the choice of individuals and organizations they used. They were prepared to try to buy the PMU, the militant Malay nationalist movement within which a still more militant and secret anti-Chinese group was formed by one of its top leaders. Those who joined this 'group within a group' were culturally backward Malays whose racial prejudices could easily be worked upon.

Yet even while Bambang Partono was trying to buy up the anti-Chinese PMU he and other Indonesians were also encouraging recruitment from among Chinese communist sympathizers too. Political extremism being what it is, these groups of opposite ideological camps were prepared to work together in their common willingness to recognize Indonesia as a friend and ally and to destroy Malaysia.

The existence of such a proliferation of small extremist groups, devoted to violence, revolution and political adventurism and romanticism, is not of course a peculiarly Malaysian phenomenon. Similar groups are to be found in almost any of the countries of Asia and Africa. The Indonesians have demonstrated how easily these may be used as a fifth column. Such groups have not, however, been composed of the sort of people who were likely to add up to a very serious revolutionary movement. None the less they have served a purpose by helping to create in the outside world an impression of discontent—even though the mass of the population has increasingly and impressively shown its loyalty to the established government.

IO

Pirates, Super-Patriots and Race Riots

A CHARACTERISTIC of the Malaysia–Indonesia–Philippines area is the existence of enormous numbers of small islands. There are 7,107 islands in the Philippines; the Indonesian archipelago has 10,000. These are strung out in such a way that the islands of one country in the area frequently come within 10 miles of the coast of another. This factor was exploited by Indonesia in the West Irian campaign when small islands near to West Irian were used as training bases and jumping-off grounds for the invasion. The Rhio Islands, which come within a few miles of Singapore and the coast of South Malaya, have been similarly used. Other Indonesian islands have been used for attacks upon Sabah and Sarawak. The islands have served Indonesia well in other ways, too.

It is possible to hop from one to another in small boats. This, despite marine police patrols, has encouraged the growth of barter trade, both legal and illegal, between the various countries and across their invisible borders.

Also characteristic of the area, and related to this, is a tradition, still very much alive, of smuggling and piracy. Often it is, to say the least, difficult to draw the line between smuggling and barter trade. For example, barter trade, so far as Singapore, a free port, is concerned, is legal. But the Indonesian traders with whom Singapurians have traditionally bartered are seen by their government as smugglers, people engaged in an illegal traffic, bringing dutiable goods into the country illicitly.

This has meant that around the coast of Indonesia and Malaysia hundreds, and possibly thousands, of small craft

95

have come and gone, operated by men engaged in illegal activities or operating on the borderline between legality and illegality. Such men are vulnerable. They are in constant danger of arrest by marine police. Almost inevitably, in the no-man's-land of the island-studded channels of the area there has been corruption. Indonesian naval personnel, marines and others, have at times themselves engaged in smuggling.

An Indonesian marine police patrol which encounters men operating small craft in which smuggled goods are hidden may seize the boat, impound its contents and have those responsible imprisoned. Or a deal may be made, there and then, about which no one will be the wiser.

The smugglers are vulnerable to blackmail, too, and subject to pressure from those who can extract a living from them in the name of 'protection'. This form of pressure is all the easier because the man engaged in illegal traffic can be disposed of at sea and no questions will be asked.

The 'Crush Malaysia' campaign had not very long been launched when an increasing number of acts of piracy by Indonesians began to be reported. A small boat from Malaya or Singapore would be seized, its crew might be thrown overboard, or just disappear. As Indonesia put economic pressure upon Malaysia, so the inducements increased. Indonesia's ban on luxury goods has made the barter trade even more worth while. Even so, this was not enough in itself to explain the fast-mounting volume of violence at sea.

Malaysian government circles claimed that these acts of piracy were deliberately encouraged, if not planned, by the Indonesian government. Again one's natural reaction was to feel that the Malaysian government was for its own propaganda purposes 'blaming everything on the Indonesian government'.

As confrontation developed, however, the evidence accumulated that the Malaysian government's charges were well founded. Among the trained terrorists in Singapore and, later, among invaders sent by sea and air to the Peninsula, were people whose stories gradually filled in useful background. Malaysian barter traders, for example, when challenged by Indonesian marine police patrols, had been offered the alternative of imprisonment (and of seizure of their vessels and cargoes), or recruitment into some terrorist organization. In other cases they were told they must assist in taking members of such organizations across to the Rhio Islands for training or in bringing them back, but without being told the purpose of their missions.

Boats used by landing parties in Johore and Malacca have in a number of cases been ones which had earlier been captured from Malaysians, thus making still more difficult the job of detecting possible landing parties, a task which would be difficult in any case with so many small craft coming and going in the normal course of events.

These various attempts to use terrorism to spread alarm and disorder were largely frustrated by the security authorities. But the quality of the human material used for subversion helped at times to reduce the operation to near-absurdity. There are, for example, a number of well-authenticated cases of near-criminal elements in Singapore who, learning that the Indonesians were looking for saboteurs and terrorists, took the explosives and the generous cash payments offered, threw the TNT or hand-grenades at the first object they came across, or just dumped them and then gave themselves up to the authorities and cheerfully went off to a two-year prison sentence, knowing that they now had a nice little sum salted away for use after their release.

Others whom the Indonesians used believed in something, but had not been given sufficient training, or perhaps lacked the intelligence, to do an effective job for their cause.

Singapore's notorious Chinese secret societies, like the Mafia of Sicily, have relatively respectable origins, far back in the past. Today they are up to the eyes in gangsterism and every sort of protection racket. Where there is lawlessness there are financial pickings for the secret societies. They thrive on violence. For this reason there has for long been a link between them and the boatmen engaged in smuggling—particularly opium smuggling.

So into the disturbed situation created by the confrontation campaign have moved the secret society men, prepared to sell themselves indiscriminately to anyone of either side. Almost by definition, they are up for sale. The Indonesian government bought them wholesale.

They have shown themselves quite prepared, for a fee, to bully and blackmail Malays and their fellow Chinese, simple fishermen, into acting as couriers between members of terrorist organizations in Singapore or the Peninsula and those who direct them from Indonesia. They have bludgeoned fishermen and barter traders into hiding volunteers and large quantities of explosives in their boats. By now there is incontrovertible evidence that what at first looked like rather far-fetched Malaysian 'war propaganda' about secret societies being used by the Indonesian government was based upon facts.

*　　*　　*

Perhaps the most disturbing form of activity into which Indonesia and its agents have gone has been the deliberate fomenting of racial hatred in a multi-racial area which until now had set an example to the world in racial harmony. Side by side with this, and related to it, has gone the attempt to drive a wedge between the Singapore government and the Central government.

The most prized possession in any kampong house today is the transistor radio. You will find it standing on a table in the place of honour. When it is not in use it is, as likely as not, covered with the very best piece of cloth the kampong dweller possesses. Over the radio come the announcements which are of vital importance to the people in their work. The people listen to it and they accept what it says. The transistor radio brings into the kampong the voice of Government, of authority. For this reason the transistor radio can be a particularly powerful weapon in the psywar.

Many of the people living in the coastal regions of Malaysia are nearer to Indonesian territory than to the nearest big Malaysian town, and so can get the Indonesian radio programmes more easily than their own. So from hitherto unimportant and obscure local stations are now beamed programmes directed not at the local Indonesian population but at the listeners just across the water, or across the border, in Malaysia. When these unsophisticated people listen to Indonesian propaganda they regard it as the voice of authority.

A study of the monitored transcripts of broadcasts from some of these stations suggests a deliberate intention to create racial conflict and disorder. In Malay language broadcasts Indonesian newscasters and commentators set out to inflame Malays against their Chinese neighbours. In Chinese language broadcasts they incite the Chinese against the Malays. For such a public the propaganda does not have to be very subtle. Envy and suspicion are easily aroused and exploited. If racial hatred can be created and whipped up into violence in places like Britain and the United States, then we have no reason to be surprised that it can also be done in Singapore.

* * *

Much of the Indonesian radio propaganda which preceded Singapore's first race riots in July 1964 took the form of branding Tunku Abdul Rahman's Alliance government, despite the fact that it is strongly Malay in composition, as being in the pocket of the Chinese. The clear aim in this case was to create suspicion of the Central government in the minds of Singapore Malays, and to play upon racial and religious prejudices in order to do so. Here are a few examples from broadcasts in the Malay language:

Radio Djakarta, April 21, 1964: 'The Tunku's régime is backed financially by the Malay Chinese Association; Abdul Rahman has hence furthered the policies of the MCA to the detriment of the Malays. All posts in the important ministries have been given by Abdul Rahman to the MCA.'

Radio Kemam, March 25: 'The Malay population is of the opinion that the UMNO led by Tunku Abdul Rahman has sold the country and the people to the Chinese merchants. The Malays are forced to live in villages, while the Chinese and Indian merchants live in the towns, where they have forced out the Malays.'

Radio Kemam, April 19, commenting on the bomb outrages in Singapore: 'According to people who are anti-Malaysia in Malaya and Singapore, the bomb explosions in Singapore are the work of the PAP government (predominantly Chinese). . . . Bomb outrages were also staged in places where Malays lived. This is aimed at making the Malays hate their Indonesian brothers.'

Radio Djakarta, June 11: 'The Abdul Rahman régime has suppressed the Moslems in their own country. . . .'

Radio Kalimantan Utara ('Azahari's radio station'), July 2: 'Tunku Abdul Rahman has shown that he is not only a traitor to his people and a traitor to all humanity . . . but also a traitor to the Malay race by sacrificing their lives for the interests of his masters.'

Normally, Indonesian propaganda takes the line that Malaysian troops are all Malays and that Malays are thus being sacrificed to the Malaysia concept. But when the race riots came to Singapore on July 21, Radio Kalimantan Utara quickly jumped in with the line that: 'Some of the troops are reported to be Chinese soldiers from the Chiang Kai-shek clique in Taiwan.'

On July 17, four days before the Singapore race riots began, Radio Kemam was 'reporting' that a Chinese in the Peninsula had killed a Malay Moslem with 'a pork butcher's knife' and that Malays had been forced by the Chinese to eat pork.

Propaganda of the opposite type in Chinese language broadcasts aimed at putting the Chinese against the Malays was particularly built up between the first and second racial clashes.

Radio Djakarta, September 1: 'The sufferings and misery of the Chinese community in Singapore in the fields of trade and economy since the establishment of the neo-colonialist project of Malaysia were purposely inflicted on it. . . . The dirty policies of Abdul Rahman are aimed at suppressing the Singapore Chinese who total 90 per cent of the island's population. . . . The police are being used to suppress the Chinese, so that they will not be able to fight against the United Malay National Organization. . . .'

Most Indonesian radio stations on August 31 quoted in Chinese a statement by President Sukarno (who in the past had shown himself to be strongly anti-Chinese) calling on the Chinese in Singapore 'to fully realize the bad intentions of the Malaysia Federation and to refuse to help the neo-colonialist project now attempting to suppress them'. This had been Indonesian propagandists' theme to Singapore Chinese for months.

Simultaneously, Radio Kemam continued its anti-Chinese line.

* * *

Throughout the four months leading up to the first race riots, racist propaganda came to Singapore from all directions. For example, during March and again in June Singapore's Special Branch was reporting the recovery of quantities of anti-Malaysia pamphlets harping on the racial theme. The investigations showed that some of this material was being smuggled in from the Rhio Islands by barter traders and distributed by various extremist groups in Singapore.

Five months before the riots, reports were being received that Indonesian customs launches and naval patrols from the Rhio Islands were conducting anti-Chinese propaganda among Malay boat crews and traders visiting Singapore. On intercepting boats they would enquire who were the owners of the boats. If they were found to be Chinese, the goods would be confiscated with the comment that they would be distributed among poor Malays. Malay crews would be encouraged to ask Singapore Malays to say who ran Singapore and whether anyone had ever heard of any Malay millionaires.

Practically every small, subversive group, especially the more extreme, chauvinistic ones, went into action during this period, and by the time the riots came anyone who could possibly be used in this way was employed. Some of the leaflets they distributed and posters they stuck upon the walls of Singapore were Indonesian-produced, some were based on Indonesian broadcasts, some were locally produced. In the areas where the race riots actually began the leaflets were distributed in the streets and outside mosques in April, May and June. Those distributed among the Malays attacked the Singapore government for 'suppression of Malays and Moslems', who were called upon to 'unite to topple the PAP government'. Some threatened riots. One distributed on the day on which the riots began (the Prophet Mohammed's birthday) urged the Malays to 'unite and crush the dictatorial Chinese PAP government led by the wretched Lee Kuan Yew, betrayer of the Malay race'.

Leaflets distributed on the eve of the riots, and typical of many others, are before me as I write. They read: 'Malays Wake Up!!! Take over Singapore, your country which has been seized by Lee Kuan Yew and his friends.' And: 'We call on the Malays to free your country from the bondage of Lee Kuan Yew and his friends who have robbed Singapore which belongs to the Malays.' Lee Kuan Yew is, of course, Chinese and the 'friends' referred to are the Chinese members of his government.

As the first riots ended, the Indonesian propagandists and all their allies and agents—all those whom they had built up into a fifth colunm—went into action to produce more and bigger riots. Leaders of a Malay Moslem 'invulnerability cult' (Islamic counterparts of Alice Lenshina, who led her followers into battle in Zambia) were brought down to Singapore from the Peninsula by extreme nationalist leaders with known Indonesian connections about which in the past they had made no secret. Malay students and others in the areas where rioting had already occurred were recruited into new groups. They were warned of a coming clash with the local Chinese and promised invulnerability if they led the fight to defend their race and faith, provided they went through a certain ceremony. This included taking an oath of allegiance, drinking holy water, and having boiling oil rubbed into their bodies. They were sold red scarves with alleged talismanic properties and given copies of verses from the Koran which refer to 'invulnerability'.

The Chinese secret society gangsters moved into the new and, to them, very promising situation created by the riots. Some went around telling the Chinese people: 'The Malays are coming to attack us, we had better get away', then looted their abandoned homes. Others did a brisk trade in such 'defensive' weapons as daggers and iron rods.

The second riots started on September 2. In the two race riots which occurred in Singapore within weeks of each other, 35 people—Malays and Chinese—died. Most of these were the completely innocent victims of the racial propagandists. It was all too typical that the second riots began with an old trishaw rider being dragged off his bicycle and killed. Prior to the summer of 1964 no deep animosity existed between the Malay and the Chinese populations of Singapore. But during the riots Malay and Chinese chauvinism was inevitably sharpened among the extremists. Even so, the mass of the population remained untouched by race hatred. Many people of one race sheltered and assisted those of the other when the riots were in progress.

The July riots came shortly after Indonesia had staged its first sea landings on the Malay Peninsula; the second came just when Indonesia was engaging in its first airdrop into the Malayan jungle. Their short-term usefulness to Indonesia was considerable. They helped to divert world attention from what was now open aggression against Malaysia, which might be expected to reduce sympathy for her just when it was particularly needed. But in the longer view, they may well have harmed the Indonesian cause.

*   *   *

The struggle against colonialism has been one of the great movements of our time. It has changed the face of the earth. For anyone concerned with human freedom there is something particularly distressing about the spectacle of leaders of a nation newly freed from colonial rule consciously and deliberately creating racial strife.

In Shanghai on November 4, 1964, President Sukarno said that at the Cairo Conference of Non-aligned Countries he had been 'the spokesman of the people of all countries fighting against imperialism and for a new type of world happiness'. But the people of the Afro-Asian countries know too much about the evils of racialism to welcome its use by one of their number. This may possibly help to explain why the Conference failed to give him the support he had expected for his campaign against Malaysia.

11

Landings by Sea and Air

INDONESIA'S confrontation of the Borneo territories began with her instigating and assisting a revolt in Brunei and continued with raids across the borders of Sarawak and Sabah. In the case of Singapore and the Malay Peninsula, active confrontation began with subversion from within.

It was clearly Indonesia's intention to try to establish the nucleus of some sort of revolutionary army on the Malayan Peninsula. In Sabah, and to a lesser extent Sarawak, they had had a certain very limited success with their attempts to subvert local people of Indonesian origin. In Malaya there are approximately 273,500 Malays of close Indonesian origin, a quarter of a million of whom live in the three states of Johore, Perak and Selangor. These concentrations of people with Indonesian connections were an obvious target for subversion. But they were not an immediately rewarding one.

So it was to the Right-wing PMIP, the leading Malay opposition party, and particularly to the small 'way-out' Malay extremist groups, that the Indonesians turned for their recruits. Their plans in due course became known to the security authorities and so were frustrated almost before those who had been given training could make first moves towards implementing them. The Indonesians were also handicapped by the fact that at that time their operational bases were on islands south of Singapore and so some distance from the Malayan coast. By June 1964, however, it became known that new bases were being established on islands off the Sumatran coast, just across the Straits from the Peninsula. At approximately the same time it became obvious that in addition to the few Malay extremists and Malays of Indonesian origin who were going off for training there was a new type of recruit who might have to be taken more seriously.

In Pontian, in Johore state, for example, young Chinese members of the extreme Left, communist-directed group who had infiltrated the Labour Party quietly disappeared. At first it was assumed that they had gone into hiding, fearing possible arrest, but evidence accumulated that they had left for the new training bases on the islands off the Sumatran coast. A similar process could be observed in other parts of the State. Activity in some branches of the Labour Party and Partai Ra'ayat suddenly declined—some had even to close down—because of the sudden disappearance of the young activists who had kept them going. A similar situation was observed a month or two later in the state of Perak. If this was the new type of recruit whom the Indonesians were getting, then in a few months infiltrators of a more formidable type might be expected, for these were eager, dedicated, militant, though misguided young people who were not up for sale. In their own way they were the 'incorruptibles'. These were no riff-raff; they were the types who were prepared to live, fight and if necessary die, for communism.

That such a movement was likely to begin was obvious. It could be, and no doubt was, anticipated by the security authorities. The banned Communist Party of Malaya had issued a policy statement on September 20, 1963, which gave warning of what was to come. This illegal document attacked the formation of Malaysia and declared that the British imperialists and 'the Abdul Rahman clique' were 'the common enemy of the peoples of Malaya and North Kalimantan'. 'At this stage,' it continued, 'the task of the peoples in these territories is to overthrow the reign of this clique, smash the neo-colonialist scheme of "Malaysia" and realize National Liberation.' It stressed that to achieve the party's aim the people must 'rely on their own strength' and 'persist in a protracted and arduous struggle, armed and otherwise'. It ended with a declaration that: 'The Malayan people will continue to fight shoulder-to-shoulder with the Indonesian people and support each other in the common struggle.'

To those familiar with such documents this clearly meant that (1) the communists were calling upon Malaysians to collaborate with the Indonesians in the attempt to 'crush Malaysia'; (2) they were telling their own activists to prepare for armed struggle and that this preparation would obviously include taking advantage of the training opportunities provided by Indonesia; (3) although they were preparing to 'fight shoulder-to-shoulder' with the Indonesians and would try to get others to do the same, they recognized that for the achievement of their own long-term aims they must 'rely on their own strength' and for this, also, an 'arduous struggle, armed and otherwise' would be required.

It was also fairly obvious that the CPM leaders, who for years had been living with the 500 or so members of their old guerrilla army up on the Thai border, were not going to abandon their carefully preserved base. It would, therefore, be the young members of the illegal communist satellite organizations, and activists whom they had put into the legal, democratic parties of the Socialist Front, who might now be expected to go for training to the Indonesian islands and then come back and do the fighting.

The Indonesian government's campaign against its own Chinese population in 1958 is well known among the Chinese of South-East Asia. It is broadly true to say that the only Chinese in Malaysia who are sympathetic to the Indonesian government are the communists and their sympathizers, a few democratic socialists who are opposed to the whole idea of Malaysia and willy-nilly must see the Indonesians as their allies, and the few boatmen and traders who benefit by trade with Indonesia. Most Malaysian Chinese take it for granted that their present status and security would be lost if Malaysia came under Indonesian domination.

Since the confrontation campaign began, many Chinese fishermen have been robbed of their boats, abducted or ill-treated by the Indonesians, and this has tended to increase feelings of hostility towards Indonesia. There is therefore little sympathy amongst the Chinese population for those who have gone to the islands for training. None the less, it is certain that between May and August 1964 several hundred young communist-influenced Chinese were smuggled over to the bases on the islands off the Sumatran coast. There is evidence to suggest that the original aim was to recruit several thousand as the nucleus of a guerrilla army which would operate on Malayan soil. It seems likely, however, that public opinion within local Chinese communities, combined with the activities of the security authorities, had by August 1964 caused the flow of recruits to slow down or even to dry up.

The Indonesians' experience in North Kalimantan had already shown them that the Malaysian Chinese communists would like to have their own units within the invading forces. These would be as much concerned with their long-term fight for communism as with the short-term aim of crushing Malaysia.

That this lesson had been learned was demonstrated when the first seaborne landing party arrived on the coast of Johore on August 17, 1964. There appear to have been two Indonesian Army regulars to every volunteer. Among the volunteers were a few local Chinese. They were trained and armed but their immediate job was to act as guides for the Indonesians. Significantly the area chosen for these first landings was near Pontian, from which the largest group of Left-wing Chinese volunteers had gone only a few months earlier.

The sergeant in the Indonesian army to whom I talked a few days after he had been taken prisoner told me that they had been told at the final briefing that their first task was to establish a guerrilla base in the deep jungle. The operation was, however, poorly organized. Its success depended upon the landing parties arriving under cover of darkness so that they might already be hiding in the jungle before daybreak. In practice, although they had only a few miles to travel from their point of embarkation on one of the Indonesian islands, it was already growing light when they arrived off the coast near Pontian. An inevitable consequence of this was that they were observed. The alarm was quickly sounded by ordinary members of the public, the security forces went into action, and within a few days a high proportion of the intruders had been taken prisoner and some were giving the Malaysians details of the operation.

A little more than two weeks later, on September 2, came the first airdrop, when parties of regulars and volunteers were brought by Hercules troop-carriers and parachuted into the area near Labis, also in Johore. The proportion of volunteers to regulars was approximately the same as at Pontian. Among the regulars were members of crack commando and parachute units. A high proportion of the volunteers this time were Malaysian Chinese. They were some of the Left-wing volunteers who not long before had gone to Indonesia for training. The landings by sea and air in Johore in August and September 1964 set the pattern in this and other ways for many similar ones which were to follow.

There could now no longer be any pretence that confrontation was just a question of Malaysian freedom fighters being trained to liberate their homeland. This was open aggression with the Indonesian government committed right up to the hilt.

*   *   *

A few days after the Labis airdrop I talked to one of the rank-and-file Chinese volunteers used in this operation. Aged twenty-six and single, he came from a poor background. His education began at the age of twelve. He left school at fourteen 'for financial reasons', worked as a pineapple plantation weeder and did various other unskilled jobs. Had he not been drawn into Left-wing political activity his life could hardly have been more humdrum and uneventful. But in 1959 he had a brief period of detention for association with communist terrorists. His overt political activity had been with the Labour Party of Malaya. He was unemployed when a friend suggested that he should go to Indonesia. With no preparation for the journey, he set off with others in a sampan and was taken to one of the islands.

There the former pineapple weeder from the heart of rural Malaya was suddenly projected into a new and exciting world in which he learned to be a parachutist. A few weeks later, when he had done seven jumps, he was embarked, with a mixed party of regulars and fellow volunteers, in an aircraft and told that there would be reception committees waiting to welcome them when they jumped into their home state. He knew the area too well and too recently to suppose that this was true. I asked him what were his thoughts as he jumped. Was he still eager to be martyred if necessary for the cause? Was he excited at the possibility of being one of those who would form the nucleus of a 'liberation army'? Disillusioned by the lack of preparation he had been given and by the contemptuous way in which he had almost literally been thrown away, grateful only to be still alive, he answered woodenly, 'I thought I was going to die.'

In one of the parties parachuted into the area near Labis were two Chinese girl volunteers. One was killed during an exchange of shots with security forces. The story of the other, even in the language of the official report, is a very human one. At 'about 11·00 hours, 5 September 64' a Chinese logger who was driving his lorry along a timber track near Labis 'saw a female Chinese dressed in civvies, crying and walking along the track towards the jungle'. She was taken to a police station by the logger and later identified as a weeder in a pineapple plantation at Pontian.

'She claims to have left Indonesia for Malaya from an unknown base with 30 others', says the report. 'She was armed with a Sten-gun, four small packs of 9 mm ammunition and a dagger ... cash $250 was recovered from her person. She has not been very co-operative.'

Many of the toughest of the Chinese volunteers have, in the very nature of the case, been among those killed in action.

Some of them established a branch of the Communist Party of Malaya in the camp where they were under training in Indonesia. Even while Army officers were giving them political courses in Indonesia's brand of anti-colonialism, they were engaging in their own political indoctrination too. In their spare time they conducted classes in Marxism–Leninism and reminded themselves and each other that communism, not just confrontation, was their long-term aim. Into their communism they put all the idealism and dedication characteristic of youngsters who join communist organizations anywhere.

One wrote: 'June 14, 1964, is a date that can never escape my memory. On that day I joined the Communist Party of Malaya. . . . There are many difficulties in the present revolutionary struggle. And in the course of this struggle I have to train and study so as to strengthen myself in my ideology and my work and be firm in my proletarian outlook. In this way I can shoulder my responsibilities. Being a member of the Communist Party I have to be loyal to the party as well as to the people of my country. I dedicate my life to the cause of revolution. . . .'

From riff-raff, corruptibles, secret-society men and gangsters to idealism and dedication of this sort is a far cry. These young Chinese are the sort of human material the Indonesians have needed, the sort that could pose a far greater problem for the Malaysian security authorities. From the Indonesian army's point of view, however, there are arguments against them: they are Chinese and they are communists. The PKI might well rejoice to see them playing the leading rôle in the Indonesian attempt to create a revolutionary force inside Malaysia, but the Indonesian army and presumably most of the Government would derive little satisfaction from such a situation. Indonesian domination of Malaya, not its conquest by Chinese communists, is their aim. Faced with this problem, the Army is compelled to follow the same course as in Sarawak and spread the Chinese communists as thinly as it can among the regulars and the other volunteers.

The Chinese communist volunteers who live to tell the tale may yet prove at some future date to be a very real problem for the Malaysian government. Indonesia could for its own reasons end its official confrontation campaign, but the communists would still continue to work for the dismemberment of Malaysia and, after that, the victory of communism. It has been confrontation which has made it possible for them even to begin to think of going over to the armed struggle at this moment.

12

The Consequences

Is it just a local dispute between two South-East Asian countries who are unable to get along together? The leaders of Indonesia's 'Crush Malaysia' campaign insist that it is not. Their confrontation concept has a world-wide application, they say. It is something which all emergent countries should accept and follow. This was the gist of President Sukarno's address to the Second Conference of Non-aligned Countries.

'Malaysia', a document issued in September 1964 by the Indonesian Information Department in Bangkok, puts this most plainly: 'It must be recognized that the present world situation is the result of a violent confrontation of two diametrically opposed social forces.' These are the newly emergent forces and the old-established forces. 'Malaysia symbolizes this confrontation in South-East Asia. The struggle against Malaysia is, therefore, merely one part of the anti-colonial struggle in Africa, Asia and Latin America.'

This leaves many questions to be asked by the puzzled observer, first of which is: where does neo-colonialism end? The arguments which President Sukarno uses against 'neo-colonialist Malaysia' would appear to apply with at least equal force to the Philippines—his neighbour on the other side. Malaysia has British bases; the Philippines has more important American ones. Malaysia's agreement with Britain comes up for review every three years and may be ended after one year at the request of either party. The Philippines' agreement with the US is for twenty-five years. Malaysia's agreement categorically states that the British Commonwealth forces based on Malaysia may only be used in other parts of the area with the consent of the Malaysian government, and already the latter have shown that, in practice, consent is not given automatically and might be withheld. US agreements with the Philippines, Japan and Thailand would appear to give America more freedom in this respect than Britain has in Malaysia. The Philippines is a member of SEATO—which Sukarno regards as an instrument of the imperialist Powers. Malaysia has refused to be associated with it.

As noted earlier, any Philippines nationalist will certainly claim that the US hold on the Philippines' economy is at least as great as is Britain's on Malaysia's. This does not in fact make either country neo-colonialist. But to Indonesia it certainly does. So if Malaysia is 'successfully' confronted today, why not the Philippines tomorrow? And, since this present confrontation is supposed to be but part of the wider picture, at what point does Indonesia stop?

It has been the PKI which has so far determined which is a neo-colonialist country, used by the old-established forces to 'encircle' Indonesia. A joint statement by the PKI and the Japanese Communist Party leaders in September 1964 protested at the presence of US forces on Japanese soil and declared that 'Japan points like a gun at Indonesia'. There might be no end to this sort of thing if Indonesia were enabled to go from one success to the next.

Indonesian leaders hark back to an ancient empire, a Greater Indonesia of the past, and invoke this to support their present actions. There are many others who might with equal justification do the same—Ghana is an obvious case in point. And who knows what other old empires in Asia, Africa and Latin America the archaeologists may not unearth? There might be no end to this sort of thing either.

But the threat to small countries from this new imperialism could—as Malaysia has learned to her cost—be as great as they experienced from the old imperialism now just coming to an end.

Mercifully, the Afro-Asian nations are not prepared, as President Sukarno discovered at Cairo, automatically to accept either his confrontation concept or the arguments he bases on it. Many are showing a natural and healthy suspicion of them and where they may lead. This, they say in effect, is where we came in: we have heard all this before.

President Sukarno's picture of a world divided into two diametrically opposed groups is rather too much like the 'two camps' concept of the John Foster Dulles days, of an 'East' and 'West' forever confronting each other. This, in a new form, is a concept from which the new countries were determined to escape. That is why they are 'non-aligned'. The outcome, the cost and the consequence of Indonesia's confrontation of Malaysia may well determine whether this continues to be their attitude. It is therefore worth taking a look at the balance sheet.

*　　*　　*

What have been the consequences so far? The first to be noted is one which the Indonesian leaders did not expect and which, against all the evidence, they refuse to accept. It is that confrontation has consolidated public opinion in each of the countries of Malaysia behind both the concept and the reality of Malaysia. This was shown by the outcome of the 1964 elections in Malaya. The same is true of Singapore, where acceptance of Malaysia could by no means have been taken for granted. A by-product of this hardening of public opinion in favour of Malaysia has in both cases been that what one may call the overt extreme Left has been hard hit. Almost inevitably, though this is not necessarily to be welcomed (since new countries need a good democratic opposition almost as much as they need good government), the democratic 'legitimate' Left has been dragged down too—largely because of its opposition to Malaysia.

The Sarawak United People's Party was the largest and by far the most significant legal opponent of Malaysia in the Borneo territories. Indonesia's attempt to crush Malaysia has changed this. In July 1964 Mr Ong Kee Hui, the party's chairman, with the backing of other responsible leaders of the party, declared in a radio interview that he and his party were now 'prepared to make Malaysia work'. The attitude of SUPP to 'the Indonesian raids across the border', he said, was that 'we cannot tolerate any violation of the territorial integrity of our country. The stand we have taken was confirmed by the recent delegates' conference of the party'. He continued: 'We condemn the use of force as contained in the Crush Malaysia confrontation policy.'

Mr Ong finished the interview by affirming his party's support for Malaysia and the need to defend the country from Indonesian attack. He urged his party's members and particularly the people in the border areas to 'co-operate with the security authorities' in dealing with the intruders.

This makes nonsense of the frequently reiterated Indonesian claim that they have gone into the Borneo territories at the desire of the mass of the people there.

If this were all, the Malaysian leaders might almost be forgiven if they felt that President Sukarno had brought about, far more effectively and rapidly than they could hope to do, the basic unity of the people and peoples of Malaysia. But there is the other side to this.

Throughout the opening stages of the long-drawn-out confrontation campaign Indonesia was at least as interested in psychological warfare, the war of nerves, and in subversion from within, as she was in the attack upon Malaysia from without. Her aims and methods must leave anyone who is familiar with them profoundly disturbed. The aim has been to drive wedges between the different countries of Malaysia, particularly between Singapore and Malaya, and also between the peoples of various races and religions. This can be done in any multi-racial area. But it is just about as far from the letter and spirit of the United Nations Charter and the Bandung Declaration of the Afro-Asian Nations as one can go.

Indonesian propagandists have accused Singapore's PAP government of trying to split the Malays and have also called on the Malays to unite in revolt against it. There has been

Indonesian propaganda which said that the Alliance government in Kuala Lumpur is against Singapore because Singapore is Chinese. There has been other propaganda, from the same source, which says the opposite—that the Alliance government is in the pocket of the Chinese. The Indonesian propagandists have tried to use economic rivalry between Singapore and Malaya, and have tried too to use religious differences between the various communities. The evils of communalism, of racial and religious conflict, are already well known to the people of Asia. Yet the Indonesian propagandists have played on Malay racialist and religious sentiments and simultaneously on the economic and political fears of the Chinese minority.

It would be absurd to suppose that every incident which occurs in Malaysia is directly Indonesian-inspired. The Indonesian propagandists have only to excite economic jealousies, political fears, religious differences and racial prejudices, and before long all sorts of people with no sympathy for Indonesia are unwittingly doing their job for them.

These prejudices are precisely the ones which, in the interests of social progress and international peace, twentieth-century man is desperately and urgently trying to leave behind him—and must do if peace is ever to be secure.

President Sukarno has devoted most of his life to fighting for social progress, for international peace, and for nations to have the 'freedom to be free'. There is something tragic about the spectacle of a man who in his last years pursues along with others a course which undermines and betrays his life's work.

Until Indonesia began its confrontation campaign, Malaysia was going from strength to strength in terms of economic development and social progress. Her rate of development was much higher than that of any other country in the area and incomparably higher than that of Indonesia. This may, of course, underlie Indonesia's hostility. For Malaysia was a standing reproach to Indonesia, with its ever-falling standard of life. Little Malaysia was in no position to threaten Indonesia militarily. Economically she was already doing so, in the sense that sooner or later the long-suffering Indonesian people might tire of being told that economic progress must wait. At some point Indonesians might begin to demand to be put on the road to the conditions which Malaysians now take for granted.

Be that as it may, against her will Malaysia has now been forced to spend money on defence which would otherwise go towards social progress. Because of the defence arrangements she had already made with Britain, Malaysia's arms bill was small by any standards. By comparison with Indonesia's it was, and must remain, ludicrously small. Every extra penny spent on her defence represents an attack by Indonesia on the development of an emergent country.

In *The Diplomatist* of May 1964 Burhanuddin Mohammad Diah, one-time Indonesian ambassador in London, now in Bangkok, wrote: 'More than ten thousand people have lost their jobs in Singapore and Malaya. Hundreds of ships have been laid up because of the Indonesian blockade of the Malayan coast. . . .' That confrontation should lead to a situation where one developing country, Indonesia, can gloat over the amount of unemployment it claims it has been able to create in another developing country must surely in itself be seen as a powerful condemnation of this concept.

No matter who has lost by confrontation, the communists of Malaya have certainly gained. Militarily and politically defeated after their abortive attempt at revolution in 1948, they now talk of going over once more to the armed struggle. Indonesia's 'Crush Malaysia' policy and her training of volunteers in guerrilla warfare have made this possible. Otherwise there could be no question of the CPM thinking in such terms today.

In Sarawak, the communist organization had been building up its forces with considerable success, but it had not thought of guerrilla warfare as being possible in the foreseeable future. Then came the Indonesian-inspired Brunei revolt. Officers of the Indonesian army began to train young communists in the art of jungle war. As a consequence, Sarawak has today the hard core, some 1,500 strong, of a trained communist guerrilla army on the other side of her border. The communists are waiting till the security forces go and their opportunity comes when they will turn their country into a battlefield again.

In Indonesia itself, one of the first and intended results of confrontation was no doubt the sort of unity which can be built up among people who are being led into war. But the basic conflict of interest between the Army and the communists has been deepened. They fight the same 'foe' but for very different reasons. Each is in it to strengthen its own position. Those positions, taking the long view, are practically irreconcilable. It remains to be seen for how long the Indonesian people will prefer emotion to rice. At Cairo, President Sukarno said: 'We must understand that economic development will bring benefits to our people only when we have torn up by their roots all the institutions, all the links that make us subservient in any way, in any fashion, to the old order of domination.'

His people may not be prepared to accept this theory indefinitely. It is not one which is likely to recommend itself to the people in the majority of emergent countries. What it means in practice for the people of Indonesia, this land of immense human and natural resources, is that rice is in increasingly short supply and its price goes up and up. President Sukarno has told his rice-eating population that they must now learn to eat corn, which is neither to their taste nor, they believe, a diet suited to their climate. And it is not rice alone but all the ordinary necessities of life which are in short supply. Colombo Plan statistics show a startling and seemingly never-ending decline in the standard of life of the Indonesian people.

People who had supposed that President Sukarno had conveniently produced his theory of world confrontation only in order to justify his 'Crush Malaysia' campaign got their answer in January 1965 when he pulled his country out of the United Nations. The reason given for the walk-out was the decision to bring Malaysia into the Security Council. This was clearly no more than a pretext, for the decision had already been made fifteen months earlier when Czechoslovakia and Malaysia, after a total of eleven indecisive votes, reached with the approval of the Assembly a 'gentleman's agreement' to share the two-year term of office, with Czechoslovakia holding the seat in 1964 and Malaysia in 1965.

Indonesia's action followed logically from the view of the United Nations expressed at the Security Council by Dr Sudjarwo in September 1964 and by President Sukarno in Cairo the following month. In short, it was in accord with the theory that UN is the creation and creature of the old-established forces and as such must be opposed by the newly emergent ones, with Indonesia at their head. The withdrawal from UN and its agencies, such as UNESCO, UNICEF and FAO, was at once described by D. N. Aidit as 'a bold stand, reflecting the desire of Indonesia for genuine self-reliance'. The communist leader expressed the hope that 'all countries of the new emerging forces will take concrete action to put an end to the imperialist-dominated UN'.

It is only the communists who stand to gain by such a situation. Their gains have already been considerable. They have good reason to like confrontation and to wish to see it continue. The membership of the PKI continues to rise. Their position with the Government has been strengthened. Sooner or later they hope to be able to use confrontation against their opponents at home as well as those abroad.

In order to be able to carry into effect his theory of continuing and widespread confrontation, President Sukarno has put his country more and more in debt as he has acquired enormous quantities of arms, aircraft and submarines from the Soviet Union. This has meant that as his country's economic position has worsened so he has been made more dependent upon Russia. This was until recently very much according to the desires of the PKI, which can claim considerable responsibility for the situation.

When Mr Mikoyan, the Soviet trouble-shooter, went to Djakarta in the summer of 1964, at the height of the Moscow–Peking controversy, it is reasonable to suppose that he reminded the Indonesian leaders of their dependence upon the Soviet Union, for they have sought to take all they could from Russia while aligning themselves with China.

This has, however, led to Indonesia's domestic and foreign policies being directly affected by the Moscow-Peking dispute. Unable as yet to provide aid to developing countries on a scale comparable to that of the Soviet Union, and anxious to keep them out of Russian hands, the Chinese have taken to preaching 'self-reliance' to them instead. They did this first in North Korea and North Vietnam. In due course they began to preach the same doctrine to the non-communist emergent countries too. For China, this was making a virtue of necessity. Sukarno, at Aidit's prompting, seized upon 'self-reliance' and made it fit into his world confrontation concept. If the new countries are really to prevail over the old, they cannot be dependent upon them.

In Djakarta's Bung Karno stadium, on the evening of January 7, 1965, announcing Indonesia's withdrawal from UN, the President told 10,000 cheering people that 'those nations which have been injured and attacked have all become powerful. The People's Republic of China has been injured and attacked, but now she has become even more powerful. The Democratic Republic of Vietnam has been injured and encircled, but she has become even more powerful. The Democratic People's Republic of Korea has been invaded and attacked, but she has become even more powerful. The Indonesian Republic is being injured and attacked, but she also becomes even more powerful.

'On the other hand, those nations which are fed by others become weaker and weaker and it is more and more impossible for them to be self-reliant. Let all of us Indonesian people stand together with the new emerging forces to overcome difficulties, crush imperialism and colonialism and smash all foreign military bases in any area!'

A joint statement, issued in the names of the Chinese and Indonesian governments on January 28, 1965, declared that 'no peaceful co-existence is possible between the new emerging forces and the old-established forces.'

China's gospel of self-reliance is intended to free new countries from both Western and Soviet influence and so to throw them into closer association with Peking. This has certainly been achieved in Indonesia's case. D. N. Aidit, as we have seen, quickly followed Sukarno's action in pulling Indonesia out of UN, with a call for the ending of the 'imperialist-dominated UN'.

The Chinese had until then usually contented themselves with denunciations of the United Nations as American-manipulated and with calls for its reorganization. But on January 24, 1965, at a banquet for Dr Subandrio, who was visiting Peking, Mr Chou En-lai, the Chinese Prime Minister, said that 'another United Nations, a revolutionary one, may well be set up'.

The probability is that the Chinese see a 'poor man's United Nations' as little more than a means of forcing the reorganization of the present UN. To Sukarno, its creation would be the point at which the new emerging forces would really begin to confront the old ones on a world scale. Meanwhile confrontation leads Indonesia into a position where she is likely to be more dependent upon China and increasingly identified with Chinese communist policies. Indonesia's position in a Peking-Djakarta axis would be that of Italy in the Rome-Berlin axis of the past, with Sukarno cast in the rôle of Mussolini. This, it will be recalled, proved in practice to be one of growing frustration and final humiliation.

But there is no conflict between Moscow and Peking so far as the need to crush Malaysia is concerned. Each for its own reasons welcomes the Indonesian campaign. This is a point at which the foreign policies of Russia, China and Indonesia meet.

Confrontation puts this 'non-aligned' country into a position of dependence upon the communist great Powers. It has led the US, which was prepared to assist the country's development, to come, in a limited way, to Malaysia's aid instead. Because of confrontation, there are more British and Commonwealth troops in South-East Asia than before it began. And Australia, Indonesia's near neighbour, has been prompted by confrontation into introducing conscription. None of these consequences is in President Sukarno's interests. They are to his loss.

Important as is the continued existence of Malaysia to the stability of South-East Asia, what is immediately at stake is whether one country has the right—on the basis of its own theory of what is or is not a free country—to invade the territory of another, smaller one in an attempt to impose its will upon it and to dictate its policies and form of government. Indonesia claims quite specifically the right to dismember the Malaysian Federation, to attempt to bring down the Alliance government, and to have a say in who should be its successor. This is something which is full of meaning for many a small country in Africa, Asia or Latin America which is anxious to preserve its freedom to pursue its own legitimate course regardless of whether that is popular with its neighbours.

If this 'right' to interfere were to be accepted, then many new countries would have far more to fear from their 'emergent' neighbours than from the great Powers. Even while the era of the old imperialism was ending, a new one would be emerging. When all is said and done, the hard fact is that, whatever the rights and wrongs of Indonesia's case may be, she has no possible right to have her armed forces on the soil of the Malay Peninsula, Sabah, Sarawak or Singapore.

APPENDIX A

UN and Malaysia Dispute

(Secretary-General's Report to General Assembly)

IN the introduction to last year's report I had referred briefly to the fact that I had sent a team of United Nations officials to carry out certain tasks as envisaged by the three governments of the Federation of Malaya, the Republic of Indonesia and the Republic of the Philippines.

On August 5, 1963, those Governments had requested me to ascertain, prior to the establishment of Malaysia, the view of the people of Sabah (North Borneo) and Sarawak within the context of General Assembly Resolution 1541 (XV) Principle IX of the Annex: 'By a fresh approach which in the opinion of the Secretary-General is necessary to ensure complete compliance with the principle of self-determination with the requirements embodied in Principle IX.'

From the very beginning of 1963 I had observed with concern the rising tension in South-East Asia on account of the difference of opinion among the countries most directly interested in the Malaysia issue. It was in the hope that some form of United Nations participation might help to reduce tensions in the area and among the parties that I agreed to respond positively to the request made by the three Governments.

As is well known the United Nations Malaysia mission expressed the opinion that the participation of the two territories in the proposed federation, having been approved by their legislative bodies, as well as by a large majority of the people through free and impartially conducted elections in which the question of Malaysia was a major issue, the significance of which was appreciated by the electorate, may be regarded as the result of the freely expressed wishes of the territory with people acting with full knowledge of the change in their status, their wishes having been expressed through informed and democratic processes impartially conducted and based on universal adult suffrage. I accepted this view of the mission in my conclusions.

Unfortunately the hope I had expressed that the participation of the United Nations might help to reduce tension has not been fulfilled. There have been continued incidents in the area and accusations and counter-accusations have been exchanged culminating in the complaint by Malaysia to the Security Council in September, 1964.

After a number of meetings the Security Council was unable to adopt a resolution on this issue.[1]

Tension in the area especially between Indonesia and Malaysia continues to be a source of concern to me.

I wish to express the hope that the endeavours of statesmen in the area to solve this difficult question peacefully will be steadfastly continued and that the leaders of the countries involved will spare no effort to bring about a peaceful settlement of their differences.

[1] The resolution specifically deplored 'the incident of September 2, 1964' (Indonesia's parachute landings on to Malaysian territory). The voting was 9 in favour and 2 against. For the resolution: Bolivia, Brazil, France, Ivory Coast, Morocco, Norway, Taiwan (China), UK, USA. Against: Soviet Union and Czechoslovakia. The Soviet Union used its veto so that no action might be taken.

APPENDIX B

Cost of Living: Retail Prices in Colombo Plan Countries
(Consumer Price Index numbers 1956 = 100)

Country	1961	1962	1963	1964 Jan.	Feb.	March
Burma (Rangoon)	103	101	99	100	100	101
Ceylon (Colombo)	100	101	104	106	106	106
India	108	112	115	120	122	123
Indonesia (Djakarta)	209	582	1254	1947	2366	2568
Korea	121	129	156	182	195	199
Laos (1959 = 100)		134	256	401	445	473
Malaysia (1960 = 100)	100	100	103	104	104	103
Pakistan (Karachi)	105	104	105	107	109	109
Philippines (Manila)	105	111	116	123	123	123
Thailand (Bangkok)	101	105	105	103	105	105
Vietnam	108	111	119	119	120	119

Source: *United Nations Monthly Bulletin of Statistics.*

APPENDIX C

The Bandung Declaration

THE ten principles on the basis of which 'nations should practise tolerance and live together in peace with one another':

1. Respect for fundamental human rights and for the purposes and principles of the Charter of the United Nations.
2. Respect for the sovereignty and territorial integrity of all nations.
3. Recognition of the equality of all races and of the equality of all nations large and small.
4. Abstention from intervention or interference in the internal affairs of another country.
5. Respect for the right of each nation to defend itself singly or collectively, in conformity with the Charter of the United Nations.
6. (a) Abstention from the use of arrangements of collective defence to serve the particular interests of any of the big Powers.
   (b) Abstention by any country from exerting pressures on other countries.
7. Refraining from acts or threats of aggression or the use of force against the territorial integrity or political independence of any country.
8. Settlement of all international disputes by peaceful means, such as negotiation, conciliation, arbitration or judicial settlement as well as other peaceful means of the parties' own choice, in conformity with the Charter of the United Nations.
9. Promotion of mutual interests and co-operation.
10. Respect for justice and international obligations.